**A Gift for You!**

Color this bookmark and cut
it out to mark your place as
you journey through

### *The Gift of Inspiration*
### *for Women.*

You may want to affix it to a
piece of cardstock and
bedazzle it in your own
beautiful way.

Enjoy the journey!

# The Gift of Inspiration for Women

### A Daybook By

## *Dream*STRONG™

### With
## Connie Gorrell
### &
## Thirty-Two Inspiring Women

A *Dream*STRONG Daybook

*The Gift of Inspiration for Women*

Printed in the United States of America
Compiled by Connie Gorrell
Cover design by Elaina Lee

ISBN-13: 978-0998265100
ISBN-10: 0998265101
Library of Congress Control Number: 2016917476


Published by: Inspirations International
P.O. Box 6, Woodburn, IN 46797
www.inspirations.international

If you are unable to order this book from your local bookseller, you may order it directly from the publisher.

Creative Works to Inspire the World

# DEDICATION

For every woman who refuses to give up on her dreams regardless of what life throws at her. For her that offers inspiration simply by being herself. Stay the course. You are truly our heroines.

With love and dedication to all parents who have lost a child. May we honor their legacies proudly.

To Rob
To Aaron
To Mike
To Nick

The dream lives on.

07-11-17
To Brad & Lisa
Thank you for being great bosses! I appreciate our friendship and pray God will continue to Bless you & Your family

Erma Bombeck says:

*"It takes a lot of courage to show your dreams to someone else."*

We say:

*"Show us yours, and we'll show you ours!"*

—The Inspiring Women of the
DreamSTRONG Foundation

# FOREWORD

## BY JULIE ANDERSON

ome of my earliest memories are dreams. By that I mean, I have always been a dreamer. Day and night.

I used to look at dew drops sprinkled across the backyard for hours when I was a little girl. Barefoot, ants marching up and over my toes, my eyes stayed focused on the droplets. In them, I saw a magical world. For me, they were the diamonds that the fairies deposited just for me in the small hours of the morning.

In my teens, I would lay on my stomach in the cool of our living room, listening to jazz pianist Keith Jarrett play the ivory keys, over and over again. While the music entranced me, I would gaze into the eyes of my teen crush, Rob Lowe. He was a mainstay in Tiger Beat Magazine in the early 80s. Keith carried Rob and me along the river of love. I had my first kiss during that time—it was a dream, but it felt real. Yes, it was Rob. He kissed me full on the mouth right before Keith finished delivering in the music what he could not say in words.

If I think long and hard about it, I stayed in a trance-like dream state from the age of five until I was seventeen. Then, just like in a fairy tale, I started living the dream. My life changed overnight. I went from a small town little girl to a big city young woman. In hindsight, way too fast, and not properly equipped, but never the less, I lived the dream.

I can tell you many stories about my life, unfathomable; some would break your heart. Those stories, the ones that are heartbreaking, almost broke me. The sting of their reality hurt so bad that I stopped dreaming.

I shut down.
I quit believing.
I almost stopped living.

There is something to be said about a dreamer's heart and their will to live. A dreamer is sensitive; a conduit for other's emotions, a giver of love. If a dreamer is not cared for correctly, just like a delicate flower, her dreams shrivel up one by one, until all that is left is a remnant of what once was.

Maybe fairies do exist after all because one day, the day that should have been my last on Earth, I was saved. From then on, I have been building myself back up. Putting the pieces together, watering myself because no one else has the ability do it the way I need it most.

Pieces, yes I was in pieces. Broken bits of a puzzle, thrown up in the air, found strewn across forty-plus years of memories. Therapists tried to help me. Friends tried with thoughtful words to sooth me. My family tried to understand me. It wasn't until I started sharing my heart, my feelings, my thoughts, and my pain with a select few that I began to heal.

Dreams returned to me when I listened to the words of encouragement from those that love me.

Words are significant.

They say that what is said cannot be unsaid. I believe that to be true. That is why I choose my words carefully and pick the ones that come from a place of love. With love, hope thrives.

Hope grows dreams. Dreams become a reality if you believe.

I believed in my dream. Other soul searchers grabbed onto my dream's tail and what was once a mirage has become tangible. ***Feminine Collective***, the website and online community, was born from my desire to be understood. Caressed by the knowledge of shared experience and raised aloft by the sharing of untold truths, I find myself in awe every day.

When I choose the content for Feminine Collective, it is my pleasure to get to know each writer's personality. I realize that what makes us different makes us the same. I am humbled and honored to be entrusted as a vehicle of deliverance for stories that have lived in the hearts and minds of this growing tribe of brilliant writers. When the publish button is pushed, and the honesty of the brave authors hits the internet, I swear I have known no sweeter joy.

I guess all of my dreaming turned me into a Dreamweaver. Finally, I am proud of who I am as a person. Remember what the Bible says, *"It is better to give than receive."* Amen.

Dream strong, have faith, speak words from the heart.
Never give up, or in.

I promise what you truly desire will come true.
Dream on, sweet dreamy girl; you got this.
Yes, you do.

Julie Anderson
*Supermodel, Creator & Publisher of*
*Feminine Collective*

## Connect with Feminine Collective on Social Media:

www.femininecollective.com

Facebook: @TheFeminineCollective

Twitter: @femininecollect

# DREAMSTRONG, DARLING

nce upon a time we were children. The promise of our lifetimes reached out before us—our hopes, our dreams, and our aspirations were yet to be claimed. We didn't hesitate to dream big. We built our castles in the sky and, to us, there was no other way to dream! There were no limitations placed on our little shoulders and there wasn't anything we could not conquer as long as we had imagination, a cape, and a popsicle. As kids, we didn't need permission to dream big—but we did need to be encouraged. We still do. My question is: Are we born inspired? If not, where do we find it, and when did we lose it?

In times of great change comes great opportunity. We may feel slightly unsettled in our life's situation, but that is nature's way of intuitively telling us that great change is coming. We struggle to keep the peace, search for solutions, pay the bills, and hold on to our safety and sanity; something—*anything*—to cling to. We struggle to surround ourselves with familiarity—especially when everything around us seems to be falling apart. Perhaps they are actually *falling into place*.

Allow me to introduce myself. My name is Connie Gorrell and I am the founder of the DreamSTRONG Foundation, a public charity dedicated to the empowerment of women and girls. My colleagues and I lovingly refer to this initiative only as *DreamSTRONG*. To me, that says it all. A new mission was born from the ashes of great change in my life.

Between the years 1999 and 2008 my husband and I endured the traumatic losses of all four of our sons—my two, and his two. We were a family blended from our first marriages, as so many are these days. Four separate incidences brought tragic news delivered to us again and again. And again. Each time our lives were turned upside down by unexpected news of another death. Shock after stunning shock. Our lifetime of dreams was shattered. As in the song *The Impossible* Dream, I couldn't bear with unbearable sorrow or run where the brave dare not go. To dream after incomprehensible losses? Impossible. My list of impossibilities seemed endless.

Building a new future from the bottom up meant there were choices to be made, possibilities to be created, and lost dreams to be found. But while dealing with sadness and deep bereavement, I allowed my body to become very ill. I am living proof that grief can kill you if you let it. Battling illness taught me the significance of self-love and self-care. Admittedly, it took me a while recognize it. I suspected that I must be a slow learner.

One winter day I surrendered to my fatigue and took an afternoon nap. In a dream-state I clearly heard my oldest son's voice say, "*Dream STRONG, Mom.*" I sat straight up, suddenly recalling a poignant conversation that took place shortly before he died at age twenty-four.

We had been discussing our individual hopes and dreams when Rob asked what I wanted to be when I 'grow up' (something I never intended to do, by the way). But that day, my thoughts silently trailed back to when my boys were small. How I wished I had done things differently when I had the chance— how much better our lives might have been had I not lacked the courage to stand in my own painful truth and admit that I had been in dire need of a life overhaul. My marriage to their father was unhappy, but I wanted to keep my family intact. I was too stubborn to acknowledge the pain I was inflicting on myself and my children by staying in that relationship.

As the conversation continued, Rob asked the ultimate question: "Mom, what do you *really* dream of doing?" He genuinely wanted to know. So, I shared my secret. I dreamed of writing for publication and having a successful business of my own someday. Then, as an afterthought, I added that I wanted to find a way to inspire women in tough situations to fight for their dreams and make a better life for themselves and those they love. He paused, and then he spoke. I will never forget Robbie's solemn words to me that day:

> "*Whatever it is you're dreaming of doing, Mom, you have to be strong—and go for it.*"

And so it is: *DreamSTRONG*.

Today I know it is possible to *DreamSTRONG* and I am asking that you embrace this for yourself, too. In your own unique way. There is great importance in having a coordinated effort to help those struggling behind us. We face tremendous stressors every day of our lives and many times we become overwhelmed. Some of us become expert actresses, living a double life, insisting that everything is fine and refusing to grab the life vest, even when it is within reach. That helps no one— not us, and certainly not those we love that are trying their *best* to love us *back*!

Keeping up appearances takes its toll physically, emotionally and spiritually, though only subtly at first. I learned that if I was suffering silently and inwardly, those around me were suffering, too. Everyone pays the price when you suffer in silence—your spouse or significant other, to be sure, but more significantly, your children. I recognized that I could never go back and change my life's circumstances but, by God, I could be a voice for others going through similar situations. Dreams and aspirations do not need to lay on hold in a quiet corner of our distant memory. I know one thing: dreams never die. They are as close as the beating of your heart. Nothing—*nothing*—is impossible for a determined woman. She only needs encouragement and a little bit of inspiration. Thus, *The Gift of Inspiration for Women.*

Right now, somewhere, there is a woman living in a similar situation as I had been those years ago. She struggles on a daily basis to wear a brave face while secretly falling apart. She may experience the emotional gamut; everything from feeling slightly unsettled to full blown chaos and in need of calculated change in her life. To her, dreams are merely visions one has at night while sleeping. She deserves a fighting chance. We all do.

Every day, I want you to ask yourself:

- Will I do something today to make my world a better place or will I choose to add to aggravation already present?

- Will I practice peacefulness or add to the stressfulness?

The more we buy into disapproval, the more we disapprove. When we engage in the act of judgement, we become judgmental. Conversely, when we focus on kindness, we are able to practice gentleness, and acceptance. The choice is ours, every new day.

## How to Use This Book

This daybook, *The Gift of Inspiration for Women,* is your daily dose of insight, support and companionship. Read it from the beginning or open to any page, any day, and you will find a unique and loving message waiting for you there. From a spirituality standpoint, there is something for everyone within these pages. It is filled with insight, poetry and hidden jewels between these covers. Find yours and mark them to read over and over again. There are journal pages in the back to list the page numbers of your favorites and to make notes.

These passages were written by thirty-two astonishing women from around the world with wisdom and life experiences they are willing to bare and share, each with a unique path behind them. They clearly understand the challenging times that propel us into new levels of loving and living. We know that it's all about the connections we make in life and it is for this reason we decided to include their individual contact information should you wish to reach out to them.

For your convenience, we have placed prayers, meditations and reflections at the beginning to make them easy to find. Another section at the end includes seasons and holidays, too.

Delight in this beautiful gift book and share its wisdom with others. Enjoy the surprises we've tucked inside for you. You will find beautiful mandalas to color throughout and a gift bookmark on the front page, thanks to Dajon Ferrell. There are meaningful messages whispered to you within these pages; I know you will find them. It is no accident that you have in your hands *The Gift of Inspiration for Women* right here and right now.

We are with you—we are a sisterhood. Live freely and joyously in confidence knowing that you are never alone. Know that you must, in your own way, **DreamSTRONG!**

With My Love and Brightest Blessings,

*Connie*

For more information on the *DreamSTRONG*™ Foundation, visit www.dreamstrong.org and join us on social media at Facebook.com/dreamstrong.org

# MEET YOUR AUTHORS

It is with great pride that present the authors of the new DreamSTRONG Daybook, *The Gift of Inspiration for Women*. Sprinkled throughout the pages of this book, they share their pearls of wisdom emanating from their hearts to yours. Here you can put the author's face to a name and reach out to them or learn more about them, if so guided. Are you ready to meet them?

***Amanda Lee*** has a Master of Arts Degree in Adult, Community, and Higher Education from Ball State University, Muncie, Indiana. She and her wonderful husband, Shawn, have seven children. When Amanda and Shawn are not traveling or spending time at the football field or on the soccer pitch, she enjoys cross stitching and crocheting. Amanda has a personal connection to DreamSTRONG. Her lifelong friendship with honoree and foundation legacy, Aaron, is forever cherished. Connect with Amanda at adlee8@bsu.edu.

***Annie Jarrett-Keffeler*** and her husband, Ryan, live in rural North Dakota. Annie is the owner of The Journey Home with AJK which provides Reiki energy therapy for humans and animals. She assists people in their journey of self-discovery and helps them connect with their own unique gifts. She is an author and the founder of A Moment of Freedom, an equine therapeutic riding program which will provide individuals the physical and emotional benefits in the utilization with horses. Connect with Annie on Facebook at The Journey Home with AJK or email her at thejourneyhomewithajk@gmail.com.

**April Dodd** is an inspirational speaker, Executive Coach, compassionate life coach, award-winning actress, and author. With a master's degree in Spiritual Psychology, April serves as a trusted confidant, guide, and partner in co-creating transformational possibilities with children, professionals, and life enthusiasts. April currently resides in Chicago, IL and creates new possibilities every day with her husband, Paul, and their two children. Connect with April at aprildodd.com or email her at april@aprildodd.com.

" *Keep Thinking Good Thoughts!* "

**Beth Robbins Bontrager,** author of *Butterfly Hugs*, lives in Goshen, Indiana with her husband, Marvin. In her writing, Beth uses insights from God's Word because she feels that in our ever-changing world, it is God's unchanging Truth that can give children and adults stability, encouragement and the renewed hope to live life to its fullest. Connect with Beth at bethrobbinsbontrager.com or on Facebook at AuthorBethRobbinsBontrager.

*Beth Robbins Bontrager*

**Caryl Mix** is the creator of the *See Yourself to Success System* and is a gifted accountability coach and mentor. Caryl's strategic one-on-one coaching programs help busy people that feel disconnected, depleted and overwhelmed from doing everything for everyone (except themselves) to discover their own inner strength and happiness. Her clients learn to create boundaries and understand the importance of the mind/body connection. To connect with Caryl, visit carylmix.com

Author, mentor, and speaker **Connie Gorrell** is passionate about helping women identify their personal and professional goals to find success through overcoming adversity. Connie speaks candidly to women in all walks of life and encourages them to tell their stories. She holds a Bachelor of Science degree and is a respected consultant and success strategist to her constituents on a global level. Connie is the founder and inspiration behind the DreamSTRONG Foundation. Connect with her at conniegorrell.com or on Facebook @ConnieSGorrell.

**Constance Mollerstuen** resides on beautiful Whidbey Island in Washington State. She is a licensed Heal Your Life Teacher, Holistic Wellness Coach, and is certified in domestic violence and sexual assault services. Her company, Harmony Holistic Coaching, provides programs that help children, teens, adults and senior citizens develop healthy habits and coping skills to improve the quality of their lives. Connect with Constance at holistichealingworkshops.com or email her at connie@holistichealingworkshops.com.

**Dajon Ferrell** is a military veteran who served for thirteen years. After experiencing struggles with PTSD due to military sexual trauma, she found a path of choosing meditation over medication. Dajon has taught for the Department of Veteran Affairs and speaks at conferences for entrepreneurs and veterans. Her coaching empowers people to excavate and cultivate the light and love that emanates from within. She has been featured in the Huffington Post and co-authored *The Invisible Thread*. Dajon lives in Mahtomedi, Minnesota with her 6-year-old son, Logan. Connect with Dajon at DajonSmiles.com.

**Dawn Malwin** is a certified Mind, Body, Spirit Practitioner, women's advocate and speaker who assists women in unhealthy relationships to free themselves and move forward to happier and healthier lives. She brings decades of personal experience and understands the pain from these relationships and the need for love, resources, and support. Dawn is a compassionate mother of two teens living in northwestern Indiana, near Chicago. She holds a Bachelor's Degree in Communications from DePaul University, and is an Advisory Board Member of the DreamSTRONG Foundation.

**Debbie Quigley** was born in Ontario, Canada. She is the author of *Wind Whispers*, a book of poetry filled with words to assist with loss, grief and faith to uplift your spirit, giving love and courage to chase your future dreams. Debbie touches hearts with her poetry—one reader, one heart, at a time. Her poetry is simple and real and filled with essential lessons derived from life experiences. Connect with Debbie at debbiequigley2001@hotmail.com. Find her books are on Amazon at amazon.com/author/debbiequigley.

**Edda Fretz** is a gifted poet, writer and photographer. She considers herself a visual artist since imagery flows the words onto the written page. Growing up overseas in Germany and traveling to many places capturing images of life, people and experiences, nuances of nature are deeply infused into her writing and photography. Edda's poetry has been published by Tower Poetry Society in Canada and Green Dove Poets for Peace, among others. Edda is on the Advisory Board for the DreamSTRONG Foundation. To follow Edda and her work visit naturallyonwave.com or eddafretz.com.

***Ellen Elizabeth Jones*** is a spiritual teacher, mystic messenger, speaker and author. As a compassionate and intuitive teacher, she guides her clients on their journey to rediscover their spiritual connection while learning to listen to their inner truth. Ellen transformed her inspirational life story into practical tools for others to use to grow and expand. She empowers others to embrace and trust the wisdom of their own heart, inspiring them to live a life of peace, love and joy! Connect at ellenelizabethjones.com or email ellen@ellenelizabethjones.com

***Erin Ramsey,*** author of *Be Amazing, Tools for Living Inspired,* is a nationally recognized inspirational speaker with over twenty years of service in the public sector. She is married to her high school sweetheart and is the mother of three sons and a daughter. Erin loves to read, walk labyrinths, entertain and bring people together for empowerment. To connect with Erin, visit her website at erinramsey.com where you can also connect with her on social media. To invite her to facilitate a workshop keynote address, email erin@erinramsey.com.

***Giuliana Melo*** is passionate about non-traditional healing modalities and working with angels. Her journey of walking through cancer caused an awakening in her spirit. Giuliana experienced true Grace and shares her experiences with others dealing with adversity in their lives. She is a certified Mind, Body, Spirit Practitioner and provides intuitive angel card readings and Reiki. Giuliana serves on the Advisory Board for the DreamSTRONG Foundation. To learn more and connect with Giuliana visit her website at giulianamelo.com.

**Jacqueline Lamica** is a freelance writer who began her career writing poetry and short stories for her eyes only. She was recently featured as a contributing author in *The Invisible Thread*, among other books. Jacqueline is passionate about helping people in need of understanding life's struggles. Until recently, she was a fulltime caregiver for her mother who is fighting the dreadful effects of Alzheimer's disease. Jacquie is a member of the DreamSTRONG Foundation Advisory Board. To connect with her, email JacquieJaxLamica@gmail.com.

**Krista Gawronski** is a mother, business owner, philanthropist, possibilitarian, and author. She considers herself a hopeless optimist and soul seeker and enjoys writing about love, courage and charity. She is the author of *Soul Purpose~Finding The Courage to Fly*. Her courageous tale encourages readers to follow their dreams and use their life for a charitable purpose. Connect with Krista on Facebook @SoulPurpose16 or to learn more her nonprofit, The Fabulous Women of Sonoma County visit soulpurposecouragetofly.com.

Award winning poet and author **Louise Huey Greenleaf** has dauntlessly survived the ravaging effects of Multiple Sclerosis since 1981. Despite being confined to a wheelchair, Louise uses her love of writing by sharing her heartfelt words of inspiration, especially to those living in adverse situations such as her own. She embraces her challenges through faith in Jesus Christ and celebrates the stillness in her life by sharing her stories and poems. For more information on Louise's published works, she may be contacted at louisehgreenleaf@gmail.com

**Megan Moffitt** is a visually impaired, gifted writer from northern California. Her passion is fiction, but has written newspaper articles as well. Megan's latest creative endeavor is writing and programming interactive text adventure games. She enjoys attending meditation sessions at the Buddhist temple and is a trained Reiki Master. Her heart's dream is to make a difference in the world through writing and energy work. Connect with Megan on Facebook at Author Megan Winter Moffitt.

**Melissa Kim Corter** is an author, Certified Hypnotherapist, Shamanic Healer, and Elemental Space Clearing™ Practitioner who helps others release fear and clear emotional clutter from their life. Through various modalities, coupled with heightened intuition, she connects with her client's spirit for expanded truth and guidance on shifting limiting beliefs. The earth, moon, and elements channel deeper levels of healing and connection for Melissa, stirring a passion to teach others to embrace the natural world. Connect with Melissa via her website at melissacorter.com.

**Michele Landers** is a Board Certified Life Purpose Coach, hypnotherapist and professional numerologist. She is a dynamic and gifted teacher, author and consultant on the subjects of personal empowerment and the law of attraction. Her books, *The Tao of Numbers* and *The Year of Living Miraculously* are informative and entertaining. Michele is a highly sought after media personality and guest speaker who teaches throughout the country. She helps clients gain clarity and direction in their lives and to discover their own unique talents. To connect with Michele visit michelelanders.com.

**Pat Roa-Perez** is an author and spiritual teacher on a mission to help women get back to their original self and create rich and meaningful lives. Drawing from spiritual lessons that helped her recover from depression and connect with her life purpose, she helps women eliminate the sabotaging noise in their heads that keeps them stuck and unhappy. A firm believer that women are destined to be the next guardians of the world, Pat encourages, inspires, and challenges women to take back control of their destiny. Connect with Pat at reinventedwomenonly.com.

**Patricia Mooneyham** (a.k.a. *The Passion Professor*) is in the business of helping women be happier by defining their own sexuality. Patricia is a native born Jersey Girl on a global mission to help women be happier and healthier. Her company, The Passion Professor, LLC, is a growing enterprise that marries spirituality, sexuality and self-respect to enhance the lives of women. Learn more at patriciamooneyham.com or connect with her on Facebook at Patricia the Passion Professor-P3. The Passion Professor reminds every woman that *Confidence is Sexy Every Day*!

**Rhonda Savage** is the Administrator for a church in Reston, Virginia. She enjoys helping others and making people feel valued. Her favorite pastime is spending time with family, especially her grandchildren. Reading and doing arts and crafts are her hobbies. Rhonda and her husband Steven currently reside in Northern Virginia but whenever possible they love to get away to their second home in Chincoteague Island on the eastern shore of Virginia. Rhonda is on the Advisory Board for the DreamSTRONG Foundation. Connect with Rhonda at rasavage54@gmail.com.

**Rowella James** channels spiritual wisdom through her writing, allowing her profound spiritual awakening to create meditations and affirmations that encourage healing through connection with the higher Source of the Universe. Rowella resides in the United Kingdom and is the author of *Fifteen Ways to Heal the World* and *From Darkness to Truth*. She is creating workshops promoting healing through art, meditation and colour therapy. Connect with Rowella at rowella.james@outlook.com or her website, rowellajames.com.

**Shelly Kay Orr** is an inspirational teacher, author and certified Mind, Body, Spirit Practitioner. Her life experiences created the passion to inspire and positively impact others. After a suicide attempt, Shelly transformed her life from one of mere existence to one of love, hope and joy. She shares her experiences of infertility, child loss, sexual abuse, suicide, body acceptance and intuitive parenting. Shelly serves on the Advisory Board for DreamSTRONG Foundation. Connect with Shelly at shellykayorr.com or email shelly@shellykayorr.com.

**Sunny Dawn Johnston** is an internationally renowned inspirational speaker and spiritual teacher. She is the author of bestselling *Invoking the Archangels: A Nine-Step Process to Heal Your Body, Mind and Soul*. Sunny founded Sunlight Alliance, a spiritual teaching and healing center located in Glendale, Arizona where she teaches classes online and onsite. Sunny is on the Board of Directors for the DreamSTRONG Foundation. She is the creator of Soul Food With Sunny, an online community and learning center, and the Detox Your Life Program, A 44-Day Mind, Body, Spirit Detox. Connect with Sunny at sunnydawnjohnston.com or on Facebook at SunnyDawnJohnstonfanpage to learn more.

**Susan M. Sparks** is the author of *The Student Life Jacket* and *Overcoming Mediocrity, Vol. III* and more. As the wife of a navy officer, she traveled to exotic locations such as Sicily and Guam, and the not-so tropical Maryland and Illinois. She adapted her talents in to work as a freelance writer, wedding photographer, Navy Public Affairs contractor, all punctuated by motherhood with a smattering of quirky gigs in between. Susan's love is working with aspiring authors and helping their dreams of being published come true. Connect with her at ASAPWritingServices.com for more information.

**Therese Taylor-Stinson** is a trained spiritual director, accomplished author, and contemplative leader with over a decade of experience. She passionately helps people live at a deeper level through contemplative prayer, fostering practices of social justice. Therese was co-editor and contributor to the groundbreaking anthology, *Embodied Spirits: Stories of Spiritual Directors of Color.* Her next volume as solo editor, *Ain't Gonna Let Nobody Turn Me Around: Stories of Contemplation and Justice*, is scheduled for release in October 2017. Email Therese at theresetaylorstinson@gmail.com.

**Toni Miller** is taking the second half of her life to come into her own. Her passion is helping others release their fears and realize just how magnificent they truly are, no matter where they are in their life's journey. Toni is an entrepreneur having owned a successful travel agency. She practices Integrated Energy Healing and is a Reiki Master. Toni is a founding member of the Board of Directors for the DreamSTRONG Foundation. Connect with her at tmmiller6711@gmail.com or on Facebook @ToniMiller.

**Tonia Browne** is an author, presenter, teacher and coach. Tonia has worked in the internationally in the United Kingdom and UAE for over twenty years. She is a strong advocate of inviting fun into our lives and encouraging people to see that there is more out there. Tonia encourages self-acceptance and her writing is interwoven with spiritual insights and personal anecdotes. Connect with Tonia via Facebook at Time4T or at time4tblog.wordpress.com.

**Trish Norman-Figueiredo** is the owner of the gift company, CuddleCube.com and a dedicated wife and loving mother of two. Trish has worn many hats in her professional life, ranging from doing what she is passionate about to what would pay the bills. She now shares her gifts and creative talents via an online care package and specialty gifts store. It is a compilation of her lifetime of personal growth and discovery. Trish has perfected the art of giving and sending a long distance hug. Visit Trish at cuddlecube.com.

**Vicky Mitchell** uses her passion for learning and helping others to activate their healing journeys by using physical, emotional and spiritual self-healing tools. She accelerated her journey of self-discovery after traditional medicine failed to diagnose her son's allergies. Vicky earned certifications at The Institute for the Psychology of Eating and at The Institute of Integrative Nutrition. She appreciates her many teachers who guided her to increase her self-love and intuition. She can help guide you on your path to increased wellness. Connect with Vicky via vickymitchell.com or email vicky@vickymitchell.com.

# SECTION ONE

## Prayers, Meditations, and Reflections to Begin & End Your Day

*The mind can go in a thousand directions, but on this beautiful path, I walk in peace. With each step, the wind blows. With each step, a flower blooms.* —Thich Nhat Hanh

# God is Love

Before you begin your day, take some time to ground yourself in Truth and take it with you into everything you do, into every way in which you show up in the world. Say these words:

God is Love
>    and so am I.

God is peace
>    and so am I.

God is kind
>    and so am I.

God is generous
>    and so am I.

God is miraculous
>    and so am I.

God is divine
>    and so am I.

God is alive
>    and so am I.

Say it until it feels real. Let it expand into all areas of you. Hold it inside of you as long as you can, without forcing it or with any attachment to what you want to happen. Move on to another area. Take the feeling with you there, and when you feel complete inside, take this expanded connection with you throughout your magnificent day.

*April Dodd*

## Morning Prayer

Thank you, God, for this day.

Let me begin by visualizing myself swimming in the rainbow-hued love of the Angels, Archangels, my Guardian Angel, and all my heavenly team.

As I move through this loving ambiance, may I feel the love and support from my insides out; let it form a protective layer around me that is as strong as steel, yet flexible enough to expand and contract as my vibrations and moods change. This shield will maintain my resolve so I can be my best version of me today.

Thank you.

Amen.

*Vicky Mitchell*

## Morning Crystal Energies Invocation

Read first thing in the morning, silently or aloud, to invite the unique energy of each stone to activate and balance the chakra to which it corresponds.

This invocation will aid you in preparing your body, mind, and spirit for handling whatever challenges may arise during your day. All seven chakras are represented, beginning with the root, followed in ascending order by the sacral, solar plexus, heart, throat, third eye, and crown.

> Black tourmaline, remind me to be strong. Remind me to be courageous as I face the uncertainty of this day. Lend me your earthly wisdom so that I may remember to stay grounded and positive, even in the midst of chaos. Shield me from negativity and keep me safe.

> Warming carnelian, send me on my way with the light of the sun shining in my soul. May I love unconditionally and show compassion to all beings.

> Sweet citrine, teach me to release my anger, and fill my aura with joy.

> Gentle rose quartz, open the gates of my heart, so that I may love myself as much as I am loved by others.

> Fearless aquamarine, inspire me to lift my voice and speak my truth.

> Lapis lazuli, stone of angels and guides, bring me peace as I move forward on my spiritual journey.

> Sacred amethyst, help me to always trust the gift of my own intuition, and to hear the divine song of the Universe everywhere I go.

*Megan Winter Moffitt*

# This Is My Prayer Today

I am reaching out to a place of peace. I have come to You, my dear Lord. Like a book with so many pages askew, so many stories wrapped up in this life of mine. I stand here and ask forgiveness for all the things I have misread, for all the times You looked at me and shook your head and wondered—*(fill in your name), why did you do that? For what means did it serve you? Do you think that was the way I would have handled it?*

I am sure that there are too many instances when I have not served You well. I ask your forgiveness, but more than that, I am opening my heart to let You in so that I may serve You in the most profound way. I only need a small push in the right direction and your loving hand to guide me through this present turmoil.

Your word and your example are like a bright light and I sometimes shy away. I need strength to be the best me and achieve to be more open to your wise words. Show me how to do this is. My prayer to You is to help me to be a better person, worthy of your love so I can continue to spread your word and give of myself in loving ways.

Amen.


*Jacqueline Lamica*

# Evening Reflection

Your life is a gift from Divine Spirit.

There is no other *You* in the Universe!

You are Truth and you are LIGHT.

Always shine it brightly by practicing kindness, forgiveness, compassion, consideration, gratitude and mostly LOVE...always and everywhere!

Start with you and let it permeate all areas of your life.

Be an inspiration to everyone you know.

This is when you are living a full life and honoring the Divine Light that connects us all.

This is Earth School—live it *well*!

If the only prayer you ever say is *thank you*, and you are truly grateful for everything and everyone in your life, then you will always have enough. Let it empower you to get through whatever life brings you and opens your heart to infinite blessings!

Say these words: *Thank you, Divine Spirit, for my life*!

*Giuliana Giuliano Melo*

# Going Deeper

Lord,

Help me to see myself clearly
in passing.

Empty me of noisy silences
that I too may find meaning
even in chaos,
that I may know the truth
regarding the kind of person I am—
the motives in my days,
the doings, and tryings, and emphases…
the values.

What is the real fruit of my sacrifice?

Does it reveal a good treasure?

Is the fruit of my harvest love?

Let my heart sing the music that comes
from deep relationship with You,
and if not, allow me to sit awhile longer in
Your Presence, until my center reflects that
with whom I have spent my time.

You, O God, do I seek!

*Therese Taylor-Stinson*

Inspired by Howard Thurman's "How Good To Center Down" *Meditations of the Heart*. Beacon Press. 1981. pp. 28-29. ©Therese Taylor-Stinson. November 2014

# Whispered Prayers

Whispered prayers and candles burning bright,
These we do together for you tonight.

Things left unsaid and so much left to do,
grief, sadness and tears are shed for you.

Butterflies, feathers, songs and coins
Are special signs—we know they are from you.
Let them remind us of the love you are.

Different now,
but with us still in spirit.

LOVE is who you are, and where you are in Heaven.
But loved and missed here forever more.

Be free.  Be free.
Let God love thee.

*Giuliana Giuliano Melo*

## Simple Forgiveness *by Susan M. Sparks*

Too often we over-complicate things. For me, forgiveness is one of those things. As a child away at camp, we'd close the evening by singing a simple hymn that began, *"If I have wounded any souls today, if I have caused one foot to go astray, if I have walked in my own willful way, dear Lord, forgive."* The tune stayed with me over the years, yet I couldn't remember all the words. Through the wonder of the internet, I found it: *An Evening Prayer*, by C. Maude Battersby.

What a discovery to find there were additional verses, just as beautiful as the first. Like a missing puzzle piece, I felt an empty space fill in my heart. As the day winds down, I find that these gentle words from my childhood summer camp can turn my focus to those who I have touched today.

> *If I have wounded any soul today,*
> *If I have caused one foot to go astray,*
> *If I have walked in my own willful way,*
> *Dear Lord, forgive!*
>
> *If I have uttered idle words or vain,*
> *If I have turned aside from want or pain,*
> *Lest I myself shall suffer through the strain,*
> *Dear Lord, forgive!*
>
> *If I have been perverse or hard, or cold,*
> *If I have longed for shelter in Thy fold,*
> *When Thou hast given me some fort to hold,*
> *Dear Lord, forgive!*
>
> *Forgive the sins I have confessed to Thee;*
> *Forgive the secret sins I do not see;*
> *O guide me, love me and my keeper be,*
> *Dear Lord, Amen*

# A Nighttime Meditation

To *you*, Dear One...

I want you to stop, right now, and close your eyes. Feet flat on the floor. Clear your mind, take a deep breath in and exhale out all the yuck of the day. Do this three times.

Everything you are worrying about is going to be okay.

It always is.

*All is well.* Worrying does nothing but make you worry more. It won't change it, it won't help it, and it won't solve it or make anything better.

The only thing that makes things better is time, faith, and wisdom to know that everything will always work out.

Trust me.

Love,

GOD

*Giuliana Giuliano Melo*

# Return from Meditation

Stay with your stillness for a moment more.

Breathe through your light with your heart and mind.

Open your spirit to the life beyond you,

Feel honesty pouring into your heart.

Be not that which you yearn for,

Strive not to attain that perfect grace.

Seek not to tie the boundaries around you,

But be still in the Light that you are.

Simply be with your Self in this moment.

Do not try to dichotomize your life

By striving to find the true self within the complexities that surround us,

But simply accept the Whole as the way you are

And the Truth will rise like a Phoenix

From the ashes of your own courageous fire.

*Rowella James*

Achieve Inner Stillness, *Fifteen Ways to Heal the World* by R. James

# SECTION TWO

## The Celebration of Courage & Inspiration Begins

*A girl should be two things—*
***who*** *and* ***what*** *she wants.*
—Coco Chanel

# Put Wings On What's In Your Heart

Have you ever admired your dreams from a distance? I have. It's not that didn't think I could achieve them; it was more that life had left me too exhausted to even try. I realized over time that I don't want to live that way. I don't want to live without a dream in my heart. I don't want to live without the faith needed to survive my sorrows with at least some sense of grace. If dreams are a reflection of the past, then grace paves the path for the future ahead.

Funny thing about grace. As writer Ann Lamott puts it, "I do not at all understand the mystery of grace—only that it meets us where we are but does not leave us where it found us." There is a glimmer of grace in every situation, but we have to look to the light to find it. Think of it this way, light trumps darkness. Always. A candle's flame lights the dark, but darkness can't pierce the light. Candles never lose their flame by lighting other candles nor are they diminished in any way for having done so.

Sorrow may be strong, but we are stronger—stronger than we give ourselves credit for, to be sure. Look for the light in every challenge. Share your stories. *Put wings on what's in your heart.*

Please don't tell me you can't do it. Tell me you're tired. That's okay. Tell me you're disappointed, disheartened or unmotivated. Got it. That's okay, too. Just don't stay there for too long. I know you wouldn't say those things to a small child or a struggling teenager, or a good friend—so don't talk to *yourself* that way, either.

Repeat this daily: The world is missing what I am ready to give. I will put wings on my dreams and make my world a better place.

*Connie Gorrell*

# Choose

Each day we have choices to make.

When we have a dream of something we want to do or be, we have choices to make that will enhance or delay the journey to that dream.

Choose to BE.

Believe in yourself. Believe in your dream. Be aware. Be in tune with the music inside of yourself. Be inspired as well as inspiring. Be confident. Be determined. Be proactive. Be a thinker of good thoughts. Be kind. Be genuine. Be true to yourself but be respectful of others. Be hope-filled. Be optimistic. Be an encourager.

These are choices that become actions which can move you forward towards your dream.

Choose this day who you want to be.
Choose wisely.
Choose to *be*.
Choose to dream.
CHOOSE.

*Beth Robbins Bontrager*

# Would You Be Surprised?

Would you be surprised
If I told you
That you are the light of the world?
You shouldn't be,
Because you are.

Would you be surprised
If I told you
That you are timeless?
You shouldn't be,
Because you are.

Would you be surprised
If I told you
That you are part of the Creator?
You shouldn't be,
Because you are.

Would you be surprised
If I told you
How beautiful you are?
You shouldn't be,
Because you are!

*Toni Miller*

# Plant Some Seeds

Seeds. Nothing holds more wonder, promise or miracles than a seed. It's amazing when you consider that you can drop a seed in the dirt, add a little water and sunshine and in a few days, a tiny green start appears. From there, it grows into a beautiful flower, nourishing vegetable or a towering tree.

Now imagine that you can plant other seeds, such as kindness, compassion and positivity. Too often we think we can only change the world with a grand gesture, but springtime can be a powerful reminder that just one tiny seed can grow into something wonderful.

What can you plant? Certainly a beautiful flower garden brings you and others joy, so plant away. But also think of what seeds you can sprinkle each day among others. Perhaps one smile won't change your moody co-worker, but it is a start. From there, you can add sunshine, water, and fertilizer as you continue to smile, say hello or pay them a genuine complement.

Just as a seed doesn't become the tree, flower or vegetable overnight, the anticipation and cultivation yields a harvest that blesses you and others.

*Susan Sparks*

# If I Were Seventeen

If I were seventeen again and took a different road,
I would not have known my sweet little girl,
So precious to hold.

If I were twenty again and made a different choice,
I would not have held your hand my son, or
Heard your sweet little voice.

If I had not changed the life I was living,
Left all my fears and hurts behind,
Then our paths may not have crossed
My husband, so strong and so kind.

If I had taken a different path or traveled a different road,
I would have missed all those moments
Of love and memories untold.

The choices I have made
Have brought me to this place.
The hurts have all begun to fade,
Because life is filled with love and grace.


*Rhonda Savage*

# Times Are Changing

Times have changed. You can no longer close yourself off and hold back—physically or spiritually. You are needed! You are in a changing time and *you* have chosen to *change* this *time*.

You have the gift! You have the knowledge! You have the wisdom! You have the awareness! You have the heart! You have it *all* within you.

When did it become okay for you to come from a place of fear? When did it become okay to hide who you *truly are* and all that you have to offer? When did you decide to allow fear to take over?

Love heals—fear harms! Are you ready to *love*? Are you ready to *live*? There has never been a more important time on our planet than now.

Listen now, and listen closely. Can you hear that soft, gentle, quiet beat of your heart? The beat that tells you that it is safe, that it is time, that all is well, and that you are ready?

Now, listen even more closely...even more closely, and you will hear them. The ones that need you. The ones that need you to share your gifts and your wisdom, your awareness. Can you hear them?

Your voices are one in the same! This voice is calling you forward...the time is NOW!

*Sunny Dawn Johnston*

## This Breath is Mine:
## An Affirmation of Ownership

This breath is my breath. Mine alone. I don't need to please anyone, do anything, or hurry in any way. This is MY breath. I can be with it in any way I care to handle right now.

There is nothing I need do to make it perfect, or complete. It is whole as it comes to and through me, and offers as much as I want to take in. I don't have to hold it. I can let go of every past breath, and enjoy all the next one brings. I can be new with each breath.

All possibilities arise as my breath does. As I breathe in, I expand all the possibilities inside and around me. As I exhale, I move this like a pulse this into every corner of my being that seeks aliveness.

I create newness with this very breath.

And it is mine to breathe.


*April Dodd*

# Dreams

She stood up wiping the dirt from her face. The grit in her mouth made her even more determined to fight. Yes, she had fallen, face first, yet again.

But this time, the fall ignited a fire within her soul. She spit out the dirt, dusted off her clothes, and with new determination burning in her soul, she turned to face the sun allowing the shadows to finally fall behind her.

Dreams.

Yes, she has dreams—and those dreams inspire her to get up, over and over; never willing to lie down in defeat.

Dreams equal hope.

Hope equals rising…again and again.

*Shelly Kay Orr*

# The Journey Home

Brick by brick, layer by layer, your house is being built.

You release old emotions, you release old patterns, making this your journey home to your house that is being built

You have carried too many burdens. You need to let go.

It is time to open yourself up to others and to receiving more of all the good things that are out there and possible for you.

Brick by brick, layer by layer, you let go—and all the while your house is being built.

Your journey home, back to you, is *you* letting go of the unknown and beginning to trust.

Lose your fear and start to have faith and little by little your journey home brings you closer to you.

And brick by brick, layer by layer, your house is being built.

You have traveled so far, this journey home. Go and live in the house that you built, layer by layer, brick by brick.

*Annie Jarrett- Keffeler*

# Faith in Moments of Doubt

I am a unique expression of God in all that I say, do and believe. I am given the ideas of creativity with all the potential to bring my dreams to life.

I believe in the goodness that I am and I trust God to fill my being with grace and the sacred truth of unconditional love.

I am free and exercise my divine right to become all that I can be. I have great support from the Spirit world and the Angels, and I am cherished in the greatest way possible.

Thank you, God, for believing in me and for always gently pushing me forward in a nurturing way. I am your truth, your light and your faith bringing this mystical, magical gift to the world in a unique way.

In any moment of doubt, I will renew my FAITH by

> **F**inding
> **A**nswers
> **I**n
> **T**he
> **H**eart

Thank you, God.

Amen.

*Ellen E. Jones*

## Float

A drop of water lands gently
forming ripples before absorption
into the total whole,
gently circling outward from the center—
a small wake flowing in a calm place, space
for floating, healing, being.

Circles of life moving peaceful,
just as ripples in a lake
easening of water with each motion.

*Edda Fretz*

*Water surrounds the lotus flower,*
*but does not wet its petals.* –Gautama Buddha

# I-AM-POSSIBLE

There are many cliché quotes that people recite to keep a positive outlook on life and their journey. Those such as, "The glass is half full," or, "When life hands you lemons, make lemonade." However, there is an affirmation in particular that not only requires one to be positive but it also incites them to invest in themselves. Simply remove the word *impossible* from your vocabulary and change it to **I AM POSSIBLE**.

Many unfavorable events are going to occur during your life journey and you have a choice to make, a fork in the road if you will, when these things do happen. Are you going to let these instances define you, or are you going to use them to make a change within yourself and ultimately, your future?

If it does not seem possible, make it possible. Begin by finding a mirror. Look straight into the mirror until you and the person staring back at you feel the drive and determination needed to push through.

Then, spell impossible: i-m-p-o-s-s-i-b-l-e.

Finally, state firmly: **I'M POSSIBLE, I AM POSSIBLE.**

*Amanda Lee*

# The Constant Companion

While tending to outside chores one summer day, something oddly caught my attention. I suddenly felt the presence of an old friend—a constant companion, a sacred sense of feminine *being*. I realized something crucial that day. I was never alone. She had been with me all along.

She is the Wind, and she whispers our name. She is that which fills the space of our existence between the heavens and the earth. We walk within her presence daily in a space where it's safe to share our secrets. As sunshine is the laughter of nature, the wind is its inspiration, the breath, and the promise of better days ahead.

She wears many faces: solar winds, trade winds, winds of change. Change. They say it is inevitable. This means our priorities must change, too. Let nature nurse you, if only for a while. When we become tired souls and weary bodies, we are not living our highest good.

Go outside. Ground yourself in nature paying particular attention to the gusts of wind that rise to meet you. Greet her face to face. She is your breath. Consciously inhale deeply with your arms open wide to embrace her; fill your heart and lung space with sacred energy. As you turn to cast your sails, feel the winds of change at your back as you exhale, releasing all that binds you to your pain or source of aggravation (if the neighbors are watching, simply smile and wave!).

Connect to your Creator and face the wind—the Breath that knew your name before your birth.

*Connie Gorrell*

# How to Trap a Monkey

An easy way to trap a monkey is to place a banana inside a staked container with a hole cut in it just wide enough for the monkey to insert its hand. When the monkey grabs the bait and clenches its paw around the food, its fist is too wide to pull its hand out. The only way the monkey can get free is to release the banana, but it won't let go, thus the monkey is captured.

Think about times when you've acted like the monkey. Holding on, attached to being right or to your possessions, judgments, addictions, distractions, attractions, pride, the past, present, or the future.

When you hold on, you have available *only* the possibilities of what is available within what you are holding on to. If you hold on to a relationship, you hold those possibilities. When you hold on to anger or regret, you hold only those possibilities.

But if you are willing to let go, open your palm and reach for the constant newness that Spirit offers, the possibilities become limitless.

*April Dodd*

# This is Your Sign!

This is your sign, dear love! Know that you are right where you are meant to be, right in the Divine time.

None of your possessions are permanent, not even your home, your body—nothing.

None of the people in our lives are separated from us. We are One. Any self-perceived separation is merely an illusion, for we are all love.

None of your confusion or worry comes from love. It's a choice derived of fear. Choose love. The answers are always within, so choose to take that journey within. Excavate through the darkness and use it to cultivate more expansion of light. Choose to shine, dear love.

Surrender your grasp. Be wild and experience the amazing freedom that comes from just *being*. No worry. No pressure. There is nothing hidden in the dark that cannot be illuminated by your light.

Take this moment to close your eyes and envision that beautiful light surrounding you. Envision the love that you are created from and for, easily pouring out of you. No attachment for there is an abundance of love within. No need to cling.

Just breathe. And *be*.

*Dajon Ferrell*

# Time Out

Just remember in the days of action and reaction there is always a minute, a moment, which exists in your busy schedule but is usually brushed aside.

Take this moment for yourself to daydream, do something fun—abstract. May your creative spirit rekindle; don't push it out of the way with excuses like "no time, tomorrow, after I do all these other things."

Don't let it suffocate—give it a chance.

Creative expression is a cleansing process for the soul which is very important especially now that all this fruitless time has gone by.

It is good to clean out the cobwebs of the mind and put into place a spring bouquet, radiant with sunshine.

Live for *yourself* through the *moment*.

*Edda Fretz*

# The Winds of Change

Growing up I was told that the universe was run by a God that wanted strict obedience or something really bad would happen. Death was the "Lord's will" and we should never question it. Watching the evening news was enough to see that bad things do happen to good people, so it was no wonder that we are all fearful. The big bad wolf does come to the door and Mother Hubbard's cupboard does go bare.

As I now know, the winds of change always blow and sooner or later that which we fear always come to the surface. When the time comes for our lives to shift, whether we are ready or not, it will be time to lay down our fear and directly face what is to come.

We need to be truly consciously aware to watch for the signs and trust that life will lead us in the best possible direction for our growth as humans. Watch and see that the synchronicities in life are a part of the bigger picture, without trying to figure out what it means or where we go from here.

We can realize that there is an intelligence in all things that helps us along the way, like a collaboration of fate. This is especially true when we have some of the greatest challenges in our life. We can never know until we stand on the mountain top and look back on things that have happened, but we can always know that if we let it, it will bring us to the top to stand in the exact place we are meant to be.

*Toni Miller*

Excerpt, The Winds of Change, *The Invisible Thread*, 2016 OptiMystic Press

# It's Okay to Have Fun!

Years ago, I went to a dear friend's home for a cup of tea. My friend, being English, had a certain way she liked to fix tea. As she prepared my cup, she added my preferred teaspoon of sugar then placed it in front of me.

As I took a taste, I silently cringed. It was horrible! I didn't want to hurt her feelings so I smiled and chatted as if all were fine. She prepared her own cup then sat across the table from me.

She took a sip and cringed. "This tastes horrible!" she said. "Why didn't you say something?" I smiled as I explained and we both laughed.

We eventually found out that her daughter had made cookies earlier that day and when she put the ingredients back in their original containers, she accidently put the salt in the sugar bowl!

It felt so good to laugh and to just have fun!

The moral of the story: Don't let stress take the joy from special moments. Let unexpected and imperfect events bring a smile to your face! Let them become opportunities where you can enjoy laughing with people around you. Give yourself permission to have fun!

*Beth Robbins Bontrager*

# Best Days Ever

What if you are, right now, living the best days of your life?

Recently I was with my new granddaughter and thinking back to the time when her dad was her age, and thinking, "Man, those were the best days ever." Funny, while it was happening so long ago, it felt like they were the most difficult. I worried most of the time, felt inadequate at best, and struggled to "get it right."

What I now realize is that looking back has given me the vantage point of seeing that I did make it through what I thought was really difficult. We survived and thrived. Everything that had happened way back then was simply preparing me for what was to come. It had allowed me to build the strength I needed to keep going.

The gift is seeing that even though things were hard, I made it through and everything is okay. Knowing this allows me the freedom to enjoy where I am today, right here, right now, because one day I am going to look back again and see that these days are, in fact, some of the best days of my life, too.

How are *you* going to make today some of your best days ever?

*Caryl Mix*

# Pathways

Many paths are made of relationships that create the map of our lives. Some roads are familiar and comforting. Some roads we think will take us onto the end of our days, and a ride into the sunset sometimes make a U-turn to a completely different direction.

There are the roads that we create and those that find their way along with us on their own journey. Some parts of the highways and byways are smooth; some are coarse and gravelly. Others remain under construction for a long periods of time until they suddenly clear then steer us to a new direction; one we had never imagined. They show us places we never knew existed— except in our dreams.

While there are times it feels the roadway is blocked, those are actually segments meant to allow us to breathe and feel the wind on our face and the sun on our brow.

Each path is part of our own journey until, at last, we rest in the shade.

*Patricia Mooneyham (a.k.a. The Passion Professor)*

# Be Extraordinary

Giving freely of ourselves without expectation or recognition is not a scary thing; an open and humble heart is the greatest gift we can give to each other. Do not be afraid to honor your joy and love. Share your gratitude, make a difference and be extraordinary!

MY words
MY choices
MY faults
MY mistakes
MY sadness
MY pain...

MY thoughts
MY path
MY merits
MY success
My happiness...

All of it is due to none other than *Myself*. If there is blame it lies solely at my feet, whereas when there is gain, this too is mine to own.

Never shrink from the challenge of being YOU!

*Trish Norman-Figueiredo*

# Be Happy!

Positive thinking is not seeing the world in a "Pollyana-ish" way. It is seeing things as they *are*. It is having the emotional resources to navigate through challenges and the ability to see what wisdom you can gain through those challenges.

The importance of having a positive attitude goes beyond feeling good. Someone with a positive attitude is less likely to suffer from stress-related illnesses, less likely to feel overwhelmed and more likely to have fulfilling relationships.

Change your attitude into a more positive one by following these simple suggestions:

- Thinking negative thoughts attract more negativity to you. When you find yourself having a negative thought, have a list handy of "what to do when I'm feeling blue" tips. When a sad mood strikes, look at the list, pick something and then do it!

- Remind yourself: *This is a moment in time, not the rest of my life.*

- Most importantly, stop the negative self talk. Saturday Night Live character, Stuart Smiley had a problem with self-esteem. His affirmation: *I'm good enough, I'm smart enough, and doggone it, people like me!* Develop your own positive self talk statement and say it daily or hourly if you must.

*Michele Landers*

# Crossroads

Standing at the crossroads of my life I want to reflect on what has become of me. I have raised my children and am happy that they have found what appears to be successful and happy lives. I have given them the tools to make good choices, what any parent would do. I look around me and see that I am independent and have a good job but all else seems a bit empty to me.

It's time to make some good choices for myself. Have you been there and wondered *what shall I do*? I am looking at the past and the present carefully, trying not to serve myself a dish of doubt and regret. It is easy to dwell on the choices we've made and wonder if we could have done more to get better, long-lasting results for the rest of our adult life.

I think that standing here at this crossroad I will choose to listen to my heart and chase the dream I once had for myself. I will write a new chapter in my book of dreams and invite you to do the same if you find yourself standing at a crossroad.

We shall be like the child who chases the elusive butterfly!

*Jacqueline Lamica*

# An Attitude of Gratitude

Several years ago I read a book about positive thinking. The book inspired me to take a look at my life and how I really felt about things. Was I a positive thinker or a negative Nelly?

I made a conscious decision to start each day by being thankful for what I have in my life. Some days I have to work a little harder than others, but soon it becomes easier and it becomes who you are.

I choose to have and attitude of gratitude:

Grateful for the gift of each day

Remembering those I love both near and far

Allowing time to laugh and play

Taking time to rest and breathe

Everyday remember to stop and pray

Facing my fears will help me reach my goal

Understanding that I can achieve my dreams

Loving with all my heart soul

*Rhonda Savage*

# Affirmations and Actions for Today

*By Vicky Mitchell*

Today, I will breathe and go with the flow through the rapids of life until I reach calm waters. I will trust the process.

Today, I will let my inner star dance while I embrace my uniqueness. I will make my play a priority.

I am the captain of my wellness team. Today, I will focus on what I want. I know that I am perfect the way I am.

I give myself permission to nourish my mind, body and soul. I make my nourishment of all types a priority in my life.

Action: Now list three ways you will achieve your affirmations and describe how you will *feel* once they are accomplished.

1.



2.



3.

# A Hero Lies in YOU

Someone called the crisis line to say they no longer wanted to live. There have been a few times in my life when I could identify with that caller. Like the day my first husband punched me in the stomach, threw me against the wall and then kicked me in the head repeatedly. Or the day that I was having yet another side effect from the prescription medication that I was taking. It was supposed to help with the depression and the Fibromyalgia that occurred after the car accident.

As I sit here today, I often wonder how I made it through those years. I kept searching for someone, anyone, to rescue me from all of the fear, trauma, illness, sadness, and despair that I had experienced for most of my life. I kept looking for validation from an outside source to make me feel important and deserving of a good life. A hero—to save me.

As I was recovering from a car accident, I learned about negative thought patterns and how they can affect your body and your life, bringing that upon which I focused into manifestation. I immediately began to change my thinking by focusing on everything I was grateful for. Thinking positively and feeling good gave me power and over time I discovered that the hero I had been searching for all along was hiding inside my own heart.

On the following page are lyrics to the song, "Hero," as sung by Mariah Carey. Reflect upon your own life to see if you can discover how to become the **HERO** you have been searching for.

*Constance Mollerstuen*

# HERO

There's a hero
If you look inside your heart
You don't have to be afraid
Of what you are
There's an answer
If you reach into your soul
And the sorrow that you know
Will melt away

Chorus: And then a hero comes along
With the strength to carry on
And you cast your fears aside
And you know you can survive
So when you feel like hope is gone
Look inside you and be strong
And you'll finally see the truth
That a hero lies in you

It's a long road
When you face the world alone
No one reaches out a hand
For you to hold

You can find love
If you search within yourself
And the emptiness you felt
Will disappear

Lord knows
Dreams are hard to follow
But don't let anyone
Tear them away
Hold on
There will be tomorrow
In time you'll find the way

Chorus: A hero lies in you

*Written by Mariah Carey, Walter Afanasieff • Copyright © Warner/Chappell Music. Inc. Universal Music Publishing Group*

# Love Yourself First, Then Others Will Love You, Too

Did you say *I love you* to yourself today? My guess is you didn't. Instead of smiling at your reflection this morning you likely picked out several things about your skin, hair or body and deemed them unlovable. Instead of being pleased with yourself as you went about your day, completing tasks, understanding other's ideas and solving problems, you probably scolded yourself for being clumsy, stupid or silly.

"But it's wrong to think of myself...I must think of others!" you protest. Yes, you do think of others, that's one of the things you can love about yourself.

Before you close your eyes tonight, tell yourself, *I love you.* How does it feel? Odd, clumsy, selfish? Good, that means you heard it. Say it again. Then say it tomorrow and the next day and the next, until it feels warm, wonderful and true.

*Susan Sparks*

# Eternal

The ebb and flow of the tide and the huge diversity of the waves mirror the relationship between the human spirit and the array of emotions we experience that appear to affect and alter who we are. Despite the weather, the moon phase or formation of the shore with which it meets, in its essence, it is still the same ocean.

Regardless of these external forces which appear to alter it so dramatically, it simply continues to expand and connect with the ether. It merges to absorb its surroundings through the eternal cycle of condensation and precipitation, yet in its essence it is still the same ocean, endlessly created anew by Source and endlessly returning to the same.

Acceptance does not mean surrender; neither does it mean complacency in challenging situations. Acceptance is finding the courage to sit tall in the presence of that which we fear the most.

*Rowella James*

## Wishes

Create a dream
make a wish
keep the faith
feed the fire of creativity.

Wishes do come true
just like the sky will
turn blue.

Chase those clouds away.
Luck will come like
another day.

Keep the faith,
feed the fire of desire.
Love will come like
ocean spray.

Washing those fears away,
Smile, it's a new day.


*Edda Fretz*

## Who We Are

We are souls visiting earth for a time. We came from the same source—from our Creator. We are here for a predetermined, yet short time. And we are here to observe, to learn, grow and heal with love. When it is time, our spirit returns to our home in Heaven.

We are each given a spark—a light, a Divine Life Force Energy. It is up to us to determine how bright we are willing to shine. The healthier we are, the brighter our light. Respect it. Nurture it.

Together our lights illuminate the earth all the way to the heavens and we shine as bright as the sun. We may feel as though our light is going out, but it never does. As long as we have breath, our light exists. Through the darkness shines the light.

The light may only be a tiny spark at times, not the big flame we desire, but it is there nudging us, softly speaking these words:

*Child, you are a part of the Sun, an unending source of Divine Light. You've got what it takes. Keep going.*

*Giuliana Melo*

# Believe in Yourself

As a young woman, I never felt I was particularly good at anything or that I was worthy. My insecurities were abundant and kept me from believing in myself.

After years of trial and error, heartbreak and tears, I knew I needed to change my thinking. I could stay where I was with a dead-end job and no prospects of a relationship or I could transform myself—believe in myself and change my thinking. Being the best was important to me, but I needed to *believe* in myself and realize that I could be good at whatever I chose to do.

This was not an overnight transformation. After some careful planning, I sold my home, left my job and moved to be near my daughter. I took time to teach myself computer skills, dressed for success, and started looking for the kind of job I wanted. I had to tell myself every day *I can do this*.

I now look into the mirror and see a confident successful woman. Start believing in yourself and know that you cannot change how others think, but you can change how *you* think!

Remember to DreamSTRONG!

*Rhonda Savage*

# Laughter Is Important

We often take ourselves too seriously. In the rush of striving to succeed, we seem to have forgotten how important laughter is to enjoying life. The push and pull in our everyday routines can stretch us to the max where stress is concerned.

Laughter can break the stress cycle and allow us to bring a new comical perspective to challenging situations.

When my mother had a stroke in 2010 and was moved to a nursing home, Mother and I made a pact to laugh even when we'd rather cry. Laughter became an important component of our coping mechanism to survive the new challenges of the nursing home experience.

In life, there will be times when we will rise to the occasion and respond to questions with classic answers and poise. Other times, because we are human, we may fall flat on our face. Learning to laugh when we would rather cry is an important technique to use as we pick ourselves up, brush off the fall, and find a way to move forward with a smile on our face.

Laughter *is* important.

*Beth Robbins Bontrager*

# Reclaiming Your True Self

From the moment we are born we are destined to lose our true identity. Slowly, the world begins to stamp on us its labels until the day we become what it wants us to be. But this false identity always falls short of who we really are, keeping us from tapping into our infinite creative power, and sooner or later we begin to feel it.

The day comes when we feel restless in our own skin, and though we do not know what it is, we feel something is missing. Something stolen from us long ago that once found will make us whole.

So, we begin our journey to reclaim what is rightfully ours (though we don't know what it is). We want more, for what we have no longer feeds our soul. Whereas a moment ago we felt slightly fulfilled, we now long for deeper meaning, purpose, and a sense that our existence matters.

For a few lucky ones, the moment will come when they realize they never lost anything and that all they have to do is reclaim their *true identity*.

And once they do, life will never be the same.


*Pat Roa-Perez*

# Robbed

I bet you were robbed today. Did you realize it? That moment when you caught a glimpse of the actress on the cover of a magazine at the checkout and told yourself you were fat, or when you saw your neighbor in their shiny new car and cringed at the sight of yours.

Comparison robs us of joy. When you are concentrating on the differences between you and that model in the magazine or the neighbor's new car, you are really telling yourself that you don't amount to much. What would you say to a robber trying to steal your valuables?

*Stop it*!

Say that to yourself the next time the comparison robber pops into your head. *Stop it*! Stop thinking that your life would be better if you were thinner, younger, older, richer. Start thinking about your valuables—loved ones, a healthy body, interests and dreams.

Next month another actress will be on the cover, and before long, there will be a newer model of your neighbor's car. What do they matter compared to those precious and dear valuables in your life? Stop comparing and start counting your blessings.

*Susan Sparks*

# Wildflower Women

There's something wonderful about wildflowers. They grace us with a vivid array of colors along our roadsides and meadows, but no one seems to notice. No matter how many times we mow them down, they return to bloom again and again. I realized something today. Life is like just like that—a wildflower.

That's when it hit me: I'm a wildflower and, come to think of it, there are a *lot* of us out there! Wildflowers are not planted, pruned or pampered. They aren't carefully fertilized nor sent to our doorstep adorned with ribbons to celebrate special occasions or milestones. They grow only with what God gives them—soil, rain, and the light of the sun. They blossom even in the most difficult of conditions, even in barren cracks along the sidewalks. Still our faith is safe and secure because we know that when they are mowed down, or the seasons change, wildflowers will thrive once again.

There are many of us in the world that show our true colors during the most difficult of conditions. We may remain unnoticed, unpampered or unadorned. We face obstacles that mow us down for the count, but not for the duration.

So here's to us, the wildflowers of the world. We grow with what God gives us—and we shall bloom once again!

*Connie Gorrell*

# Rainbows

We will always face storms in our lives. Some will come silently and others will arrive with flashes of light and the resounding clap of thunder.

But storms always pass. Weathering them bravely with our head held high allows us to see the exquisite rainbows waiting there for us at the end. Rainbows occur only in the presence of light—the essence of our very souls are light.

So when the storms of life pass on by, the light from our soul captures the luminescence of colorful prisms that cast beautiful rainbows above us. No storms ever pass without leaving behind the lesson of seeing the beauty of our own light.

The next time you see a rainbow, honor the light of your soul and the blessings of the storm.

*Shelly Kay Orr*

## Safe, Loved and Protected

Hearing the words in my right ear just before impact, "Take the hit. You will be fine. Take the hit. You will be fine. Take the hit..." are probably not your normal thoughts before a crashing impact with a semi-truck. I knew I was being Divinely guided. I was *safe*.

After feeling a tingling sensation from my clavicles up and around my head and down my neck, I knew I was *protected*.

Miraculously, my body relaxed moments before impact and my head and upper body were supported snuggly in place by who I knew to be my Guardian Angels. This 'letting go' sensation is what helped save my life. I was not in control that day. God was.

As I eased my way out of my partially crushed driver's window and realized I was whole, and I was alive, I heard God's voice for the first time, "I chose you! Now, I need you to finish!" I was *loved*.

The entire day I was *safe*. I was *loved*. I was *protected*.

I realized in every point in my life I was safe, loved and protected, and so are you.

YOU are *Safe*!
YOU are *Loved*!
YOU are *Protected*!

*Annie Jarrett-Keffeler*

# The Journey We Choose

If we all lived like there were no endings, only new beginnings, or there were no dead ends, only opportunities to forge a new path, we would live with no regrets. We would not waste our time wishing we would have said or would have done something. Instead we would say, "When we meet again..."

But until that time, we can honor and love ourselves and others enough to take more turns in our journey, make new opportunities in our life, and above all, *live*. Learn from the lessons our past has to offer and push on to create a new path, a new beginning, or continue on a path already started.

Always love deeply and completely, and push on with a smile to light your way. Let your dreams guide you through your journey.

*Amanda Lee*

# Who's Judging You?

If you think you're afraid to have, do, or be something because of what others might think of you, think again.

The only reason you worry about what others think is because secretly, you fear that the negative things you think about yourself are true. You may have convinced yourself that the judgment is "out there," but no external judgment could affect you if you held yourself in high esteem. If you truly felt one-hundred percent okay with who you are right now, then what others thought of you would have no bearing on how you feel about yourself.

When you adopt radical self-acceptance and unconditional loving towards *you*, you release yourself from the trap of complying to get others' approval.

*April Dodd*

# Abundance

You have the gift of Freedom beneath your feet—if you will only seek the Courage to breathe.

You have the fire of Passion burning in your heart—if you will only seek the Honour to let go.

You have the breath of Truth dancing within your Soul—if you will only seek the Faith to listen.

You have the gift of every moment of the day within you—the dance of your body, the energy of your mind, the wisdom of your heart, the Universal Consciousness which seeks its path within your Soul.

You have the Gift of Gnosis—a deep knowledge of what the message entails; what is needed of you tonight.

Have no thoughts but those which are sent in Spirit from beyond the stars, from the Divine Source of Inspiration.

Return in consciousness to the roots of your existence. Feel Divine Consciousness within your Soul.

Feel.
Listen.
Become.


*Rowella James*


Speak to me of Abundance, *Darkness to Truth* by R. James

# Disconnect and Re-energize

Everywhere you look today, people are connected to their electronics. Technology has become a powerful connection in our society.

Many 'connections' improve our lives, like electricity. Appliances connected by electricity work to make tasks easier. Gasoline, through the gas tank and the workings of the engine, somehow connect and power a vehicle to move forward.

It is mind-boggling to see how many people have phones in their hands (or up to their ears). Technology has taken over every aspect of our lives. With that being said, though technology can be a powerful and positive tool, it can also be a draining connection for our lives and dreams.

When we become glued to our phone, video games and computer, we can forget how to live life joyfully—and dream dreams. Staying plugged into technology 24/7 never gives our brain, hearts and souls time to disconnect and re-energize.

Dreaming dreams is powered not by electronics but by connections that we find within us. God has placed a seed of life in each of us. By connecting to that life source for our thoughts, hopes and dreams, *the light of the soul* switches on and our energy is renewed.

*Beth Robbins Bontrager*

# Celebrated Friendship

Once in a lifetime someone comes along
From your youthful past
Loving the girl you once were
Now the woman you have become.
Love is timeless and ageless with this special person
Their smile touches your heart
As it did years back!
Bringing you once again laughter
Sharing life's lessons.

This special person
From your youthful past
Loving you through the years.
Love is ageless and timeless
Your heart knows that you will always be friends
On life's path until your journey ends
God sends you a special friend in your lifetime.
This person always finds you!
To share a smile or share a tear
A special love you have year after year


Hugs,

*Debbie Quigley*

# Change the Color of Your Lens

Today is going to be the best day of your life! What can you find to be grateful for? The sun, the rain, your home, your family, your breath, the dirty dishes in the sink. Even though life may seem to be inundating you with pain and heartache, I know you can find one small thing to embrace which will bring you great joy.

When you look at life with the same lens as you did yesterday you will continue to see the same muted colors and get the same muted results. If you don't like these results, then just for today, in this moment, choose a more vibrant lens!

Ask yourself the following question: "What one thing can I do today that will bring me the most joy?"

*Constance Mollerstuen*

# Dream Strong, My Beautiful Child of the Cosmos

On this amazing day awake and know you are loved.

See magic everywhere you look.

Hear beauty in spoken words and see sunshine, even in the darkest of places.

Behold the smile on people's faces and see the sparkle in the eyes of the children.

Honor the untold stories of the old and the miracles that are and will be performed by the young.

See your breath dance and hear it sing, daring you to live, encouraging you to contribute to this world of wonder and mystery—this dimension of love.

Feel the vibrancy of possibilities, for today there is only love in action.

Review your to-do list and revise it so that at the top you write: *Enjoy this day.*

For today is unique and it invites you to DreamSTRONG!

*Tonia Brown*

# DAILY NUDGES FROM YOUR SPIRIT
*By Melissa Corter*

To get a daily nudge in your inbox, visit www.melissacorter.com

*Here are samples of your daily nudges. Enjoy!*

🦋 Perhaps it is that easy. What if the questioning and deciding what you want is the work, and the receiving of it all is the easy part? Let's find out.

🦋 Let yourself experience the freedom in trusting in the vision spirit has for you. Become the co-creator; let go of the control. Control is simply an illusion anyway.

🦋 Priorities and commitments can change. If it doesn't feel in alignment any longer, there is always a way to release it, even in contracts and agreements.

🦋 Do not let their fur, age, or species get in the way of receiving powerful messages. Spirit speaks to us in various forms.

🦋 You are a powerful creator. Learn to laugh at, be aware of, and release any of the creations that came about mindlessly. Reset your energetic alignment. Begin again.

🦋 Witness the world, yet do not invest your energy into the stories of drama, fear, lack, and separation. Unity is only a thought away.

🦋 Ask Spirit how you can upgrade your "lens" of the world. It is possible to see more love, to witness more beauty, and to be in alignment to only see the blessings everywhere? You will never know if you do not try.

🦋 Witnessing the power of your own mind is empowering. The more you practice consciously creating, the more certain lessons begin to leave your experience for others to surface.

🦋 All steps take time, each one having a different pace depending where you are in a process, in your life, and comfort zone. There is no right or wrong way, and if you are guided you may skip a step or revisit the same one over and over again. Surrender to your higher self and the evidence of manifestation will move through your life experience more rapidly.

🦋 Move past self-doubt and mental chatter; get beyond the insecurities and remember why you do what you do. You will connect with others whom resonate with you and what you believe in.

🦋 Close your eyes and imagine yourself receiving and being in the exact manifestation of what you are called to. If it is a new home, see yourself in it. If it is living without anxiety, feel the peace in your body. Whatever it is you desire, see it in your mind's eye and slowly bring in the other senses and feel it.

## I Can Be As Contrary As I Choose

I refuse to dim my light so that others may shine theirs brighter.

I refuse to let the opinion of others determine my own self worth.

I refuse to squander my personal power.

I refuse to allow past mistakes to define me.

I refuse to lay down and give up on myself—or my dreams.

I refuse to be unhappy.

I refuse to be ordinary.

I refuse to live behind excuses.

I refuse to apologize for something I did not do.

I refuse to apologize for the behavior of others.

I refuse to please others at the expense of my emotional well-being.

I refuse to stress or give excess energy to circumstances over which I have no control.

I refuse to settle for less than I deserve.

Look out world, because today I can be as contrary as I choose—and I choose to refuse!


*Connie Gorrell*

# Woman's Life Moments

Magic moments
Simple pleasures
Laughter and childhood memories
Teenage adventures life lessons
Loving another first intimate moment
Looking in the eyes of your first born
The little hand you hold
Years pass quickly
Life's heartaches and heartbreaks
Time heals the heart with aging lessons learned
Appreciation of gains in life
Shared moments with family and friends
Smiles and tears include life's moments
As we age and look back
Always things we think would like changed
Truth be known realistically
Life's moments makes us who we are today!
Love each life moment
Smile often love as much as you can
Be there for a friend on a bad day
All moments whether good or bad
Life is about magical moments
Look at each wrinkle in the mirror with pride
Each line holds a story
Love each day of life
Each stress mark and laugh line
Made you the woman you are today!
Treasure your life moments
Create new magic moments
Make your reflection of life
A woman's life you are proud of!

*Debbie Quigley*

# The Worry Fast

Fasting is usually associated with food, but how about a worry fast? There are so many things you can let go during one. For instance, did you worry more about what people thought about you, than what *you* thought about you? Are you concentrating more on the person you think people want to see than who *you* want to see?

A worry fast could be your antidote. How freeing would it be to not concern yourself with someone else's opinion of you? Frightening, you say? I know. It was for me, too. Worrying about what others think is the primary activity of a people pleaser.

Just like fasting from food, it is best to start small and work your way up to longer periods. Set a timer for an hour. Find something to work on that will keep you focused. If a worry pops up, just tell it, "Not now," and continue on. If it persists, write it down and push it away. You can even promise that you'll worry about it at 4 o'clock or in the third mile of your run. Or, you can give it up all together.

*Susan Sparks*

# This Little Light of Mine

A dream often begins from a spark that is ignited deep within us. For each person, the spark may begin differently. Perhaps a memory lights a small flame of interest or it could be an event that ignites a passion.

As I have grown older, I have realized that the light that shines within me comes from a source greater than me. As I have read God's Word, His Light that comes from the pages of His Word has helped the light within me to grow stronger. I can honestly say that HIS Strength and Truth has been the fuel that has kept the light of my dream shining. God has fueled "the little light" of my dreams through many affirmations. And, as He fueled the light within me, my dream found its identity in my writing with His Purpose in mind.

Discovery becomes a journey of personal growth when we allow 'the little light' within us to shine. Then, each step we take in life becomes illuminated so we can see more clearly the path to our dreams.

Find the spark within.

Fuel it with positives.

Then, let *your* little light shine!


*Beth Robbins Bontrager*

# The Present Moment

Today I will live my life as though it is a miracle and I will appreciate everything that occurs. Living in the present moment, being conscious of my thoughts and my feelings will guide me towards the wholeness and healing that I seek.

When you learn to break life down into small, manageable pieces it is easier to realize what truly matters. Setting time aside to reflect on where you have been and where you want to go allows the opportunity to understand who you are a little bit more. Through this understanding, you will be able to discover what you are passionate about, what you are grateful for, and what is needed for your healing.

To increase your present moment awareness, close your eyes and take a deep breath while counting to four. Hold your breath for a count of four, and then slowly breathe out through your mouth for a count of four. Repeat these steps five times.

Now, consider this: Today is the first day of the rest of your life.

How will you choose to live?

*Constance Mollerstuen*

# Inner Balance

I used to spend so much time looking for the answer to the never-ending question: How can I find balance in my work and home life and find time for myself?

Every time some catastrophe happened, I would buy another book, take another course or watch another webinar, with hopes that the answer would soon reveal itself. And it seems the more time I spent running around trying to find the answer, the more tired I became and the answer would seem further away.

It finally took everything falling apart all around me, physically, emotionally and financially for me to understand that the answer that I was looking for was already inside of me. What I needed was *inner balance*—balance within myself. When I began to create a solid foundation within myself to stand on, I was able to cope better with the chaos of life that was going on all around me. I found that creating systems for myself, taking time to rest when needed, and getting clear on what I needed and wanted were most important.

We can't control everything going on all around us but we absolutely can decide how we are going to react to it.

*Caryl Mix*

# Trust

Trust and faith are of the heart. Real security in life lies in relishing life's insecurity. When we don't trust, we try to control. *Fear* is the root of a vulnerable and insecure ego which controls in an effort to protect itself. When we trust enough to give up our need to control, we relax and open to the flow of energy. Trust is a quality of the soul; control is a tool of the mind.

By living only in our heads, we over intellectualize our emotions. We analyze, rationalize and explain them away so quickly that we don't actually experience them. We must learn to honor our emotions at all times by being willing to feel them and knowing how and when to express them.

Instead of being angry, upset or resentful when faced with an observation of your character, be authentic and true. Acknowledge that part of yourself which is less than perfect and embrace who you are.

*The truth will set you free*—and everything else will fall into place, just as it should.

*Trish Norman-Figueiredo*

## In Memory of My Grandmothers

Power makes us feel strong.

Strength gives us courage.

The choice is ours what we do with it. Each day is a choice and a challenge. Do we use our strength and courage to build up and share with others? Do we keep it to ourselves and only harbor fear? Or maybe when we share we only tear down those who we fear.

All choices come from either a place of love or a place of fear. It takes great courage to love others but even more to love ourselves. Once we have that knowledge, there are no limits to the power and courage with which we can in turn empower the world.

May each day inspire more knowledge for the true power lies in the knowledge of LOVE.

*Patricia Mooneyham*

# Be Inspired!

When we are inspired, things somehow take on a magical quality. That's how it is for me. I'm here, at least the physical part, yet my energy, my essence is communicating to me from another plane. I'm on *fire with desire* and I cannot stop the flow of ideas. We all know that feeling; we don't eat and we lose track of time and space. Hours fly by that feel like minutes.

Inspiration comes in many different ways and forms. We love to romanticize about it. We think it comes with lightning bolt force and with the sounds of harps playing. Inspiration can come with lightning speed, but most likely it comes as a whisper, not a yell. Maybe we hear it at the edge of sleep or deep within a dream. We can be doing any number of ordinary, everyday things when we feel the gentle nudging of our soul urging us to reach higher.

Know that you are unique and the world is waiting to hear and see what special gifts you have to share. Inside of you something incredible is waiting to be known.

Be inspired—today! Can you really live without knowing what inspires you? Why would you want to?

*Michele Landers*

# The Gift to Shift

What if I told you that you are doing a lot better than you think you are? We can all take comfort that the Universe is quietly following us through our journey. Yes, it is offering us gentle wisdom every single day. It may surprise you to learn that messages may come through loved ones, spiritual signs, and meaningful life lessons. Sometimes the messages are just faint whispers that can only be heard in silent moments and in prayer.

Our life experience will deliver love and wisdom in the most profound situations. It certainly raises the question: *Are you paying attention?*

It's true—the Universe will shake us by the shoulders from time to time begging us to notice something, someone, or just our own reckless behavior. We sometimes forget that the Universe is working in our favor. It will invite us to shift our priorities. It may be a shift in our attitude, or a shift toward love, forgiveness, or self-care. Although it may be difficult to see right away, these moments will open our eyes to a new way of being present, mindful, and grateful. We must remember that our peace and our joy can only come from deep within our own soul. Just for today, challenge your heart to listen.

Where are you being called to make a shift in your life? On some level, you already know.

Peace and Kindness,


*Krista Gawronski*

# Don't Postpone Joy

It was a stormy day and I was stuck in the Chicago airport. It was hard to keep my thoughts positive and my presence peaceful amongst crowds and frustration. Out of the corner of my eye I saw a man's t-shirt that said "Don't Postpone Joy." I asked where he found his shirt. He told me that the t-shirts were made in honor of his friend. He had a friend named Joy who was killed in a car accident in her twenties. When she was alive she would say, "Don't postpone joy," so they made the shirts for her funeral.

**Life is short. We are meant to live joyously.**

By using your thoughts, you can choose where to focus. Things like traffic, bad weather, and negative people are often used as distractions and joy drains. The trick is to focus on yourself and how you perceive each moment and situation. When you have opportunity to do something fun seize it. When you see something funny let yourself laugh. Keep focused on gratitude and courage and the power you have to make joy a current reality.

*Erin Ramsey*

Excerpt from *Be Amazing, Tools for Living Inspired* by Erin Ramsey

# Seeing Through a Child's Eyes

While driving to our little vacation spot at the beach, my youngest granddaughter who was with us spoke up and said, "Nana, did you know your eyes are like cameras? If you see something pretty, you just blink your eyes and make a picture in your mind." Wow, out of the mouths of babes.

Now, as I drive or walk along, I look around and take pictures with my eyes of the beautiful trees, flowers and clouds in the sky.

On another drive to the island, it was raining quite a bit when suddenly there appeared the most beautiful rainbow...and then another!

My sweet granddaughter looked up and said, "Rainbows are special, just like unicorns." She asked, "Nana, do you believe in unicorns?" I said of course, as she proceeded to let me know only those who believe in them can see the unicorns. To most people they just look like regular horses. So, we looked for unicorns all weekend on the island with the wild ponies.

The moral of the story: Use your mind to picture your dreams, because dreams are like unicorns—you have to believe in them to see them.

*Rhonda Savage*

# The Truth About Purpose

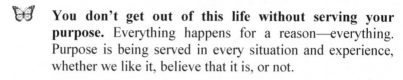 **You don't get out of this life without serving your purpose.** Everything happens for a reason—everything. Purpose is being served in every situation and experience, whether we like it, believe that it is, or not.

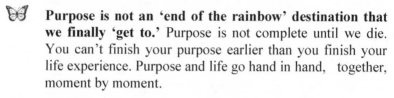 **Purpose is not an 'end of the rainbow' destination that we finally 'get to.'** Purpose is not complete until we die. You can't finish your purpose earlier than you finish your life experience. Purpose and life go hand in hand,   together, moment by moment.

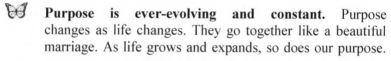 **Purpose is ever-evolving and constant.** Purpose changes as life changes. They go together like a beautiful marriage. As life grows and expands, so does our purpose.

**Purpose is a lifetime journey.** Purpose does not end. Even when this physical journey ends and we go back into spirit we are still purposeful. We are just not living, physical beings.

**Purpose is not a grandiose thing that only the successful people experience.** Purpose happens. Regardless of what our perception of someone's life experience is, it is their purpose. Different areas of the world experience life differently. Every one, in every way, is serving their purpose, even if it is seemingly difficult to look at.

**Purpose is innate.** It is who we are, who we are meant to be at any given time. You can't run away from what is within you! You are spirit embodied. *And so too is your purpose, dwelling within.*

*Sunny Dawn Johnston*

Excerpt from *Living Your Purpose* by Sunny Dawn Johnston

# The Wisdom of Freedom

Be like the birds in their joyous flight. Live freely with abandon, but may your abandon always be rooted in a sense of purpose and faith.

Soar and rejoice in your freedom, but do so in the knowledge that you are not one but instead a part of a greater synthesis between humans, animals, sunsets and stars.

Harness the energy to encompass the Divine, acknowledging with pure faith that we are sparks of consciousness within a perfect and enlightened Universe.

Thank the Ego for the protection which it serves but trust that from now on it may always be guided by the Soul.

Bury your feet in the Earth for you never know when you may need them.

Feel the vitality of the Earth spiraling upwards through your body while the light of heaven nurtures your soul from above.

Remember always that you are a child of the Earth, carrying your own fragment of God within your heart.

Know this, and your Freedom will follow.


*Rowella James*


Bless Me with the Wisdom of Freedom. *Darkness to Truth*. R. James

# Now I Know

One of my favorite daybooks of all time is *Simple Abundance*, written by Sarah Ban Breathnach. The original version of this book was given to me as a gift when it was first released in the mid-nineties. Since then it has wildly resonated with women around the world creating the demand for several updated printings and translated into multiple languages. It goes to show that we, the women of the world, are more alike than we are different.

Here is my favorite passage. Well, one of many. It speaks to me greatly and I want to share this jewel with you. I hope it speaks to you as well. Take heart of this message:

> *I wish I had known from the beginning that I was born a strong woman. What a difference it would have made. I wish I had known that I was born a courageous woman. I have spent so much of my life cowering. How many conversations would I not only have started, but finished if I had known I possessed a warrior's heart?*

> *I wish I had known that I was born to take on the world. I wouldn't have run from it for so long, rather I would have run to it and embraced it with open arms. Now I know.*

Sarah Ban Breathnach

Now *you and I* know, too!

*Connie Gorrell*

*Simple Abundance: A Daybook of Comfort and Joy*, Breathnach, Warner Books

# The Tangled Web

Being human can be challenging. Dealing with the twists and turns that life takes from birth to death can test the determination of the strongest-willed person. We begin life being born into different circumstances which become our first reference points.

Hurts, joys, lessons taught by family, as well as lessons learned by life experiences, all become mixed into the tangled web of reference points which define us. In society today, many values have been repurposed to meet the "wants" of a new generation.

Basic human reference points such as kindness, respect and compassion have gotten tangled into a larger web of new attitudes. When we find ourselves caught in such a tangled web of 'stuff,' how can the dreams we have inside survive?

1. Seek a quiet place to de-stress from the noise of the world. In the silence we can find the reference point of *calmness*.

2. Seek to renew your mind. In the pages of God's Word and inspirational authors we can find snippets of wisdom to renew *hope*.

3. Seek to be kind. In setting ourselves apart from the crowds filled with anger we can show *compassion* by planting seeds of *kindness*.

Then, DREAM STRONG!

*Beth Robbins Bontrager*

# Millions of Reasons to Smile Today

It seems evident that our lives are beyond busy these days. We're jam-packed with endless responsibilities and exorbitant activities that we are losing touch with taking just a snippet of time to relax our minds and nourish our souls with the simple and abundant gifts that are *everywhere* around us. Take in and enjoy!

As we waken this morning
let us mindfully pray,
for some millions of reasons
to smile today.

An abundant buffet
clad from heaven above,
overflowing and bursting
with God's Holy love.

For each leaf on each tree
may *all* count as one,
every bird that flies by
and the warmth of the sun.

To each whom we meet
let us greet with a smile.
Take a peek at the clouds
even just for a while.

Vision strawberries, butterflies, prayers,
children laughing, rainbows, puppies,
and flowers in bloom.
Poetry, music, elderly wisdom,
a stroll in the park in the cool afternoon.

All wondrous gifts
like the coo of a dove,
just as *everyone's* smile
is laced with God's love.

Then when the day ends let our memories portray, *all* those millions of reasons we smiled today.

*Louise Huey Greenleaf*

# The Gift of Balance

You can learn to find balance in your life. Touch, breathe, live from the Divine Source; but remember that your feet sink into this Earth each day when you walk and that it is the cool breath of scented air and the warm radiance of the sun which keeps your body alive and full of vitality.

Maintain great connection with the Universe beyond; fuse with the Divine Source and become the Creator within your own Creation. Root yourself firmly as the tree grounds its roots within the earth, for within the Earth itself is the essence of Divine Source. We do not need to seek it for it surrounds us every day.

*Rowella James*

Instill within me the Gift of Balance, *Darkness to Truth* by R. James

# Finding Center

You know that feeling you get when you can't figure out what's wrong and everything seems really hard no matter what you do? You're exhausted, nothing brings you joy, your whole body hurts, your family says you're ignoring them and you wish you had someone else's life.

For me, that's what happens when life is out of balance and I've lost my center. Dedicating too much time to one area of our lives causes problems in other areas. Living a balanced life means that all areas that are important to us get equal attention.

Are you living a balanced life?

1. See the circle on the next page.

2. Label the sections in the circle to reflect each important area of your life (family, career, self-care, etc.).

3. On each of the inside lines make 10 small marks to represent the numbers 1-10. Closest to center is 1.

4. Make a dot on each line in each category to reflect your level of happiness in that category (1=low, 10=high)

5. Draw a line connecting the dots, making a new circle.

Is your circle perfectly round? If not, why? What are some things you could do in each category to improve your life's balance?

*Constance Mollerstuen*

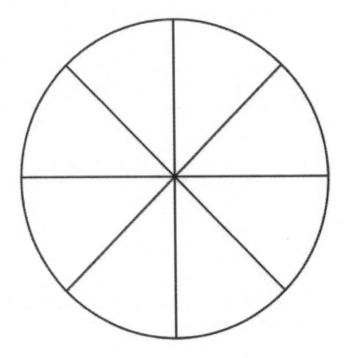

**Thoughts:**

# What Are You Holding Onto?

Recently I was having a conversation with a client. She was very frustrated at not being able to follow through on the last half of her goal. She was almost there, but couldn't seem to cross the finish line.

Have you ever had that happen where you know what you have to do, you have already had some success, but are finding that you just can't seem to pull it together to finish it up? What gives?

I asked her, "What are you holding on to?"

When we are reaching for something, we need to reach with our hands wide open to be able to grab onto the next rung or whatever it is that we are reaching for. When we find ourselves unable to grab hold of the next rung, typically it means that we are holding onto something else, making it impossible for us to reach out. A tightly clenched fist can't reach for or grab onto anything. She could very easily see that she was clutching fear, uncertainty and lack of clarity very tightly.

The next time you are feeling stuck or can't move forward, ask yourself this: "*What am I holding on to?*"

*Caryl Mix*

# How Is It?

How is it that when someone breaks your heart, your love for that person continues wholeheartedly, amidst the tiny shards?

It is because there is no greater bliss than pure and honest love; no greater gift than being able to give of it unconditionally—accepting that one's dysfunction cannot be fixed by another's love and empathy. Self-pity, anger, guilt and insecurity must heal from within.

Knowing that life is infinitely good amid its up and downs and its twists and turns, it is through our faith in hand, our heartfelt smiles, and abundance of love we shall always dwell in the peaceful knowledge that goodness prevails.

This allows us to share our heart, even when it's been broken...

It is God's gift to us.

*Trish Norman-Figueiredo*

# I Love You to the Moon and Back

*I love you to the moon and back...*

Simple words shared between mother and child. Yet, the depth is infinite. The distance to the moon is mystical and exponential for a young child, very much like a mother's love. But how does one measure it? How would you get there, let alone all the way back? Seems impossible perhaps even unfathomable to a small child.

As we get older some of these questions get answered, but that simple phrase is said with love to encompass all the amazement, hope and limitless possibility of the blessing a mother sees in her child. The endearment encompasses the unconditional being, the creative capability and the mystical bond of a mother's love.

> May today be all about unconditional, limitless, breathtaking—LOVE.

*Patricia Mooneyham*

# My Wish For You

That you find that person who hugs you on good days
and bad ones!
A person that loves who you are!
Is the shoulder you cry on and lean on
A person that never hurts your feelings
Makes you never feel lonely
Shares your laughter
Shares your dreams
Is proud of you each and every day
With whatever accomplishments you make
Or strive for!
Holds your hand on the dark days and on the light
ones!
One that promises hold true!
My wish for you!
They are always that warm hug
One that holds you and your heart
My wish for you!

*Debbie Quigley*

# Take Flight

Oftentimes we, as travelers, wander aimlessly down each path, fumbling and tripping through the rough journey we have encountered. Most of us do not realize that there is an alternate path—a path that will allow you to soar above the hardships and struggle. More so, we do not have to make this journey alone.

It does not make you weak to look around and seek assistance from those around you. Many times you will find that they have learned something from their experience that can help you with yours. Do not struggle when there is a friend offering you an out-stretched hand.

Together you can combine your experiences and journeys, rise above the rugged path, and take flight to your final destination. And the best part is, you will not arrive alone.

*Amanda Lee*

# The Brush of a Breeze

I feel the brush of the breeze on my cheek and in gratitude, my face moves toward the sun.

I feel warmth of the sun on my face and when I'm lost in that feeling, the breeze calls me back.

I stop, take a deep breath, and listen to the breeze that blows...

It makes the trees, the grass and the all the crops and fields talk.

It tells me secrets; it whispers answers to questions I have.

It calms me; it makes me stop and I ground myself to Mother Earth and I listen...

Do you hear it?

Do you feel it?

It's gentle; it's washing away what needs to be let go of.

The breeze cleanses me so that I may start fresh, and in gratitude, my face moves toward the sun.

*Annie Jarrett-Keffeler*

# Wild Gratitude

It seems we are experiencing some very scary times. You might ask, "How can I possibly be happy when (*fill in the blank*) is happening?"

There are many ways to raise your level of happiness. One concept—one virtue—outshines them all. It's something I call *wild gratitude*.

Wild gratitude is unrestrained, uninhibited deep reverence for the things in our life that we so often take for granted. It is much more than appreciation. Look around you at the natural miracles that abound in your life: the bright blue sky, the vast ocean and breathtaking mountains. You think this is just another day in your life? It's not. It is a gift and it deserves the reference of wild gratitude.

Wild gratitude urges you to be grateful for all things, at all times. What that does that look like: *Be grateful for all things, at all times*? You are grateful your friend didn't die; if they do die, you are grateful that you knew them. You are grateful for what has happened, and grateful for what has not happened.

Practice wild gratitude by listing all the challenges in your life today. Dig deep to find the gift in these challenges.

Practicing wild gratitude will change your life, I promise!

*Michele Landers*

# I Am A Writer

This label surprises me, and many people, because I struggled with several unique ways of learning as a child. Often I heard, "You are a poor reader and writer." In fact, the dean of my college called me into her office and told me that she was concerned about my abilities!

Such beliefs about my writing were a strong counterforce, even when I was invited to write. For example, friends would tell me I needed to write a cookbook. For a long time, I lacked confidence and ignored the desire to write.

However, I finally listened and trusted my intuition. When a friend shared an opportunity to contribute to a book, I took a deep breath and followed my belief that I had a message to share. I wrote my chapter. My assistant and editor helped me fine tune it. I was so proud when I received positive feedback from the publisher.

So yes, I am now a published author and I want everyone with a learning uniqueness to know that you are more than someone else's label—you have a story to share.

If you believe it and feel it, you can take action, get support, and create it!

*Vicky Mitchell*

# Amongst Friends

In the embrace of tall, leafy trees

and under the blanket of a cool starry night sky,

they gather around an open fire.


A coming together of friends

to form the unspoken bond formed long ago.


An informal ritual

guided by the strength of night

~ a womanly time.


A bewitching feeling stirred the senses,

laughter, closeness,

a mission of unity and secrecy

shared through unspoken words.


*Edda Fretz*

# My Own Prison

Life is filled with the consequences of the decisions that you make. At times you are proud of what you have chosen, but sometimes you are ashamed. Inner turmoil, stress and fear live hidden below the surface. Unconsciously you will leave a mark through an outer manifestation of your self-imposed prison. Coming to terms with this reality can unlock the door and guide you towards another level of healing.

Clutter is an outward expression of the inner chaos that you feel. When you can't resolve things that are bothering you they will manifest elsewhere. You may notice clothes laying all over your bedroom, piles of papers or, like me, your drawers can be disorganized and stuff shoved into closets.

Take a close look at your home—inside and out. Now take ten minutes to write down what you notice. Is there clutter all around or hidden away? Are you feeling stress, exhaustion, or have an illness? Clean one small area every day or once a week. Notice what comes up for you.

Freeing yourself from the confines of your self-imposed prison releases energy back to you. Healing will occur and you will find more joy and enthusiasm for life.

*Constance Mollerstuen*

# When the Mind is Stuck

When your mind gets stuck replaying a scenario over and over again, like a broken record, it can make you feel sick, frightened, worried, or hopeless. When this happens, remember that you are never *really* stuck—you've just been busy holding on to something that you consciously or unconsciously valued at some point.

Want to know what you've valued up to now? Take a look inside and around you. Your current reality reflects what you have valued in the past. To create a life that aligns with who you are today, you must detach from what you no longer value. Want to shift your reality? Try this simple, yet powerful exercise:

> On a sheet of paper, draw a vertical line down the page at about the one-third mark and another about a third over from there. In the first third, write, draw, express everything your mind is stuck on. Don't hold back, and don't edit.
>
> In the second section, write what you would *rather* be putting your attention on. Don't hold back, and don't edit. Cut along the line between the first and second sections.
>
> Burn the first section, while saying, "I give thanks and declare this complete."
>
> In the final third, ask yourself this question: *Who do I need to be in order to put my attention on a new focus?* Remember, we become what we focus on.
>
> Post the second and third sections in view and use them as your daily mantra, intention, prayer, focus of energy, and ideal life scene from which to take your next unlocking actions

*April Dodd*

# Your Prescription

Health insurance, co-pays, in-network providers. Just trying to navigate the system seems to cause more discomfort. We don't need a doctor to write the prescription—we really need an hour of trees, breezes and bird songs.

Parks have benches for a reason. You need to stop and sit down. Now, breathe. Breathe again. Try it one more time with your eyes closed. Don't worry about looking silly. Chances are the other people in the park already know the treatment. That's why they are there. Close your eyes, pick a sound and concentrate on it; the rustle of the leaves, a bird singing or a babbling brook. Feel your body relax and your pulse slow. Repeat daily, even twice daily if needed. Load up on a variety of parks, trails, gardens or even a quiet space in your back yard.

There is scientific evidence that time in nature reduces blood pressure, heart rates and stress, just to name a few ailments. What they don't tell you is that you can't overdose on it!

If you were waiting on someone to write you a prescription, then here it is:

Go outside!


*Susan Sparks*

# Kind Words

*If you can't say something nice then don't say anything at all.*

How many times have you heard this saying? I am sure we have all heard it while growing up. Words can encourage us; they can discourage us or be the difference in someone's decision to keep going or to give up.

On a beautiful summer day while I was eating lunch a young man walked by. He paused then came closer to my window. He was hungry because he had not eaten all day. He wondered if I would help him. I learned that the man was battling alcoholism and had lost everything due to his addiction. I took out a ten-dollar bill from my purse and, before I handed it to him, I said, "This is not much but it will buy you food for today. Promise me you will keep seeking help. I will pray for you."

With tears in his eyes he said, "Your words are the first kind words I have heard today." He thanked me and walked away.

What effect will your words have on someone's life? Have you heard or given encouraging or compassionate words today? Your kind and encouraging words *can* make a difference.

*Rhonda Savage*

# Passing the Baton

How can we get back to simple joys?

Perhaps in our little corner of the world, it is simply living with our family in mind. Living with our families in mind is dedicating quality time to the next generation. It is telling family stories to them. It is teaching the basic life skills of cooking, cleaning and maintaining a home to the youth in our family. It is putting a loving arm around a hurting heart and encouraging them with words of hope. It is about resurrecting and teaching our children and grandchildren the basic human values of kindness, compassion, and respect.

When I think of simple joys I think of family. As a child, our family gatherings centered on conversation and not on cell phones. Our television was off and the quiet summer evenings permeated our home through open windows.

Drifting off to sleep, I would not replay the news but would look out my window and watch the glow of fireflies twinkle in the field across the street.

During those memorable times of family, my patriotism for America, my dreams of tomorrow and the simple joys of life took root.

*Beth Robbins Bontrager*

# I Have Learned . . .

I have learned that God's plans for my life are far better than mine.
I have learned that intimate relationships are difficult.
I have learned that the best way to have anything is to let go.
I have learned that my relationship with God is the love of my life.
I have learned that I possess everything I need.
I have learned that sometimes the truth is not helpful or needed.
I have learned that sometimes it is better to just walk away.
I have learned that all people possess a common humanity.
I have learned to look on everyone with compassion, but some
    people are not good for me.
I have learned that loving oneself is not optional.
I have learned that, in God's economy, generosity pays great
    dividends!
I have learned that we don't always reap what we sow.
I have learned that honesty builds trust.
I have learned that there is no faith without doubt.
I have learned that we share the air; we take a breath, without
    conflict.
I have learned that the first step in the creative process is to show
    up.
I have learned that all things are in a state of impermanence.
I have learned that the universe is an eternal process of birthing,
    correcting, refining, evolving.

*Therese Taylor-Stinson*

# Time Is...

A moment

A smile

A touch

A word

A memory

Time is a gift

Time is now

Time is a minute

Time is an hour

Time is months and years

Time is now!

Time is life each second

Each day

Each moment and memory

Make your time count

Your time is now!


*Debbie Quigley*

# Choices

I am here to tell you how perfect you are, and though you may believe that to be wrong, please listen. We are the same. You are awesome and must believe in yourself. Be proud of the accomplishments that you have achieved, even if those choices didn't come out the way you perceived they would.

The voices in our heads speak to us exactly what we give them permission to say. Have you given yourself enough credit for all the good decisions you have made? Like most of us, you may be doubting yourself. You may be saying I should have done it differently. We live and learn; we make mistakes but really, my friend, we are just learning. As a child, we had to make choices. We had no idea of the outcome, but we still went after it with complete abandon. We were learning what the world around us and how to navigate it.

As adults we begin to listen to the doubting voices of our past and caution takes control. Athletes will tell us that failure made them stronger and fueled them with urgency to push harder for the goals they wanted to achieve.

Let us look at our opportunities and step past the hurdles and be the best version of yourself—no matter the risk!

*Jacqueline Lamica*

# Touching Space, Touching Spirit, Touching Heart

Where the journey begins is in a place called within.
Deep inside where the stillness feels no breath,
hears no voices, feels no pain, just a heartbeat.

A heartbeat one at a time, the inner rhythm of life.
The inner sanctuary, a safe space, to just be,
a place for feeling, trusting, healing…
the nurturing womb for oneself.

*Edda Fretz*

# Me, Myself, and I

Me, myself, and I are separate yet together.

Is it my own strength that will pull me through to the other side of pain, disappointments and heartache, and on to a place where I can believe in myself enough so that I can dream again? Or is there something, someone, outside of me that strengthens me to do all things?

As I reflect upon these thoughts, I wonder if there is a connection to someone greater than me, myself, and I that will help me to be the best person I can be?

With time and moments of discovery, I begin to see anew that there *is* One who created a dream within me because He created me to be the best of me, myself, and I.

In all things as I acknowledge Him, I see me, myself, and I more clearly. And in that moment, I realize that the dreams within me can become a reality because He strengthens and guides me.

Me, myself, and I are separate yet together.

> *For I can do everything through Christ, who gives me strength.* —Philippians 4:13 NLT

*Beth Robbins Bontrager*

# You Are Undefined

The people you came through do not define you. Think about that for a minute. Just because you came through the parents and family you did, does not mean that you are defined by who they are.

How have you allowed your ancestral experience to define you? How much pain do you hold that's not even yours? What grief do you bear that's not yours to hold? Though you may have come through a family that held high levels of dysfunction, your job is to raise your level of consciousness and shed those stories. To do that, you must follow the calling of your soul, as it always leads in the way that has loving in it.

To be new, you must do new. To do that, simply give yourself permission to define yourself and go your own way. Do that, even once, and you will never again pay attention to the limitations of the definition with which you grew up.

*April Dodd*

# Cherokee Legend Retold

There is an old Cherokee legend of two wolves living within each of us. One is evil; she is anger, envy, sorrow, regret, greed, arrogance, self-pity, guilt, resentment, inferiority, lies, false pride, superiority and ego. The other is good; she is joy, peace, love, hope, serenity, humility, kindness, benevolence, empathy, generosity, truth, compassion and faith.

The legend concludes that whichever wolf we readily feed is the one that will prevail and dominate our thoughts and heart. It is my belief, however, that because both wolves are part of what makes us human, and they are as intricate a part of our being as the double helix is to our DNA, the two wolves can coexist within our beings because we are a combination of the spiritual and the emotional.

Our good wolf represents our spiritual self and is always at the ready to share its gifts and love, while our evil wolf is a reflection of our emotional self and is ruled by our ego and psyche. Learning to embrace, and not fear, either of our two sides is key to living our journey to its fullest.

Seeing ourselves for who we truly are, in our entirety, our good and our beautiful, our bad and our ugly, will allow us to accept and embrace all that we are and help us to bring our shadowy selves into the light.

*Trish Norman-Figueiredo*

# In Moonlight

Do not be afraid, my love,

To walk the path of your

Own private Mystery.

Seek within the courage to be bold,

To embrace the flame of Spirit,

Which guides your private Destiny.

Make Peace, my love,

With the darkness in your Soul;

For every shadow casts its Light

In the Harmony of the world.


*Rowella James*

Excerpt: Ourselves, *Fifteen Ways to Heal the World* by R. James

# A Community of Women

As a child, I remember my mother and grandmother being the nurturers of our family. Each week they would visit elderly family members. I remember how the women of the family would help get the food on the table at family meals. Then, after everyone had finished eating, the women would gather in the kitchen to clean up from the meal all the while laughing and talking with each other.

Through this community of women, I learned about life by hearing stories of "the old days" which made us all laugh and sometimes, cry. I also discovered that the beauty of being a part of this community was that both young and old had a place in it.

As time passed, many of the elderly in our family died or became disabled. During these years of change, the community of women that I once knew now became a community of ladies from our church, neighbors and close friends.

At any age, we can choose to be a part of or build a community of women—women who nurture, encourage, inspire and teach each other to live with joy and to DreamSTRONG.

*Beth Robbins Bontrager*

# From You

Dear Me,

You were awesome today. You really should be proud of yourself. You are a pretty amazing person. You cared for others, paid attention to details, and pulled more than your fair share of the load. You helped the mom with the toddler and the stroller through a heavy door, let someone else have the closer parking spot and cracked a joke that made the harried cashier smile. You really did a bang-up job!

But, I'm afraid you won't read this. Instead, you're busy rehashing the day, telling yourself that you dropped the ball somehow. Maybe you missed getting to the bank before it closed, forgot your power suit at the cleaners, or dinner was burned because everyone was late getting home. There were bills in the mail and a leak in the bathroom. All you want to do is crawl into bed and make it all go away. Before you do, go back and read the first paragraph.

Tomorrow you'll get up and do it again...and you will be awesome tomorrow, too.

*Susan Sparks*

## Connections

Looking within yourself,
seeing through the outer shell
of another.

Trusting feelings, not analyzing,
rationalizing.

Going with the flow,
being on the path which unrolls
in the present—

Now,
like a whisper in the breeze
touch-seeing with the heart.
Feeling love, connecting by heart, spirit, mind.
Journey for transformation,
healing…

*Being.*

*Edda Fretz*

# The Towel

When I feel like giving up, when life has become too much for me, when I want to 'throw in the towel' and surrender, I use that towel to help me, instead.

The towel has so many purposes and so many ways that it can help me to keep going, to begin again. I can use the towel to wipe away my tears, and absorb my pain, sadness, anger, and frustration.

I can wrap myself in the towel for comfort and reassurance. I can dry myself with the towel after I shower, washing off anything that was weighing me down. I can also use the towel to snap anything that is trying to bring me down, and it will clean up any messes that were created that day.

I can wring it out when it becomes too heavy, and wash it and dry it when it becomes too soiled. The towel will be there for me the next time I need it.

The '*Towel*' has become a source of comfort to me and I cherish it now, instead of throwing it in. The next time I feel defeated, overwhelmed, exhausted, and discouraged, I will use the towel to help me instead of surrendering it.

*Dawn Malwin*

## .•´*¨`*• ♡,•• •❥ The Woman in the Glass

When you get what you want as your struggle for self
And the world makes you queen for a day,
Just go to the mirror and look at yourself,
And see what that woman has to say.

For it isn't your father or mother or husband
Whose judgment upon you must pass;
The person whose verdict counts most in your life
Is the one staring back from the glass.

She's the person to please, never mind all the rest,
For she's with you clear up to the end.
And you've passed your most dangerous, difficult test
If the woman in the glass is your friend.

You may fool the whole world down the pathway of life,
And get pats on your back as you pass.
But your final reward will be heartache and tears
If you've cheated the woman in the glass.

*© Author: Dale Wimbrow*

# Inspire

Have you ever stopped to think about the definition of the word *inspire*? According to the Merriam-Webster Dictionary the simple definitions are:

- to make (someone) want to do something
- to give (someone) an idea about what to do or create
- to cause (something) to happen or be created
- to cause someone to have (a feeling or emotion)

Driving to work, I might hear a special song that inspires me to sing. As I take a stroll on a beautiful day and admire the sky, the trees and flowers all around me, I feel inspired to draw a picture.

What inspires you?

The archaic definition of inspire is to breathe or blow into or upon; to infuse (as life) by breathing. When someone tells us to stop and breathe they are inspiring us to be calm. By being calm we can let our creative energy flow. So therefore, we are able to inspire others.

Think about what might inspire you then take that inspiration and pass it on to someone else. You just never know what you might inspire others to do.

Take a deep breath and be an inspiration to someone today!

*Rhonda Savage*

## Radiant Resilience

A Chinese proverb reads, "The journey of a thousand miles begins with a single step." I love that wisdom of life's journey and we can all agree on its truth. But what happens when your personal roadmap becomes tattered and torn through the years? What if that same single step launches you a thousand miles away from your intended destination and into uncharted lands?

At every pivotal point in life we are forced into making choices—whether we choose to acknowledge them as such or not. In fact, *not* to make a choice *is* indeed making a choice!

Pause to mindfully embrace, recognize, and acknowledge the true radiant resilience of your sweet essence. We are indeed wondrously and uniquely made—and for a purpose. What's yours? I really want to know.

Take a peek back through your life's journey. Envision times when you radiated resilience—times when you stood your ground, though you didn't think you could. Or when you fought for something you believed in, when others thought you shouldn't. Maybe a time when you simply smiled at a stranger because something told you they needed one.

Seek yourself in the Sacred and know that by Nature—and by God—you will get through anything life throws at you. Honor your remarkable resilience and inner radiance. Let them shine and let them glow!

*Connie Gorrell*

# Tending the Fire

A fire needs tending.

If you just did nothing, it would go out!
Our relationship with God also needs tending.

God is always there, always providing a tender loving gaze.

If we do not tend ourselves to that gaze,
   we will not show the light of God's
   tender, loving gaze in our own lives.

A fire needs different forms of fuel to keep it going...
   large, solid logs; logs shaved of its
   bark, showing splinters of wood;
   kindling, paper, and the hot wood
   coals from the previous fuel.

We also need different kinds of fuel to
   tend our relationship with God—
   serious study and reflection,
   devotional material to guide our
   thoughts, daily moments of the
   ordinary, silence, prayer,
   contemplation, meditation...
A fire needs air to breathe.

We also need Spirit (ruah) to enjoy the life of the Spirit.

Fire and air are both symbols of Spirit.
Our spirit needs the spirits of others
   to give life to our relationship with the Holy Spirit.

The wood in a fire has to be turned,
   periodically, to expose the embers in need of air.
We too need to turn,
   to expose ourselves
   to places in our lives that need to breathe...
   new life and new experience
   to nurture the fire of our relationship with God.

Sometimes, you just need to step back from the fire.
   Watch how it burns...

Sometimes in our lives,
   we need to step back from our engagement with the world
   to see anew how God may be speaking...
   to our souls.

*Therese Taylor-Stinson*

# Faith

Everything in life has two forces: day and night, yin and yang, fire and water, air and earth. Without shadows we cannot perfect the dance. Where night meets day, there is the perfect pinnacle of light which bathes the land in dew and touches the wings of eagles with the promise of fire. When day meets night, the heat of the sun becomes melting shadows across the land, turning fire back into earth.

Within each moment there is darkness and there is light. As the sky around us fades to black, the light of a billion galaxies glitters above and around us. These immense and distant sources of light, unseen by the light of day, become perceptible only through the presence of darkness.

Even within the shadows of our mind, there is a light so gentle, so eternal, so certain to be seen if we can only step back and perceive it with our Soul.

*Rowella James*

Excerpt: Speak to Me of Faith. *From Darkness to Truth* by R. James

# Your Power

Are you worried that you're not contributing to the greater good since you didn't dig a well or feed orphans in Africa today?

It's easy to discount our actions when the headlines tout great humanitarian works in far flung places. Doing great works doesn't have to be overt and dramatic, for there is power in the calm, serene, and comforting spirits that performs their miracles quietly.

Listening without interrupting, offering a kind word or hug, smiling at a stranger—small, yet powerful ways to change a person's life. It is okay to be that still, serene presence that this hurried, on-line world so desperately needs.

Think back over today. Who smiled because you were there? Who said, "Thank you," to you? Who came one step closer to their goal because of your encouragement?

Yes, the world needs well-diggers and those who feed the orphans too, but your power, that calming, comforting, stillness is just as powerful.

*Susan Sparks*

# Smiles

Thank you, God, for handling all my problems today. I am a caregiver, using smiles to get me through the day. I can reflect what is in my heart but there are no words that can be spoken. She can no longer formulate the correct words that convey what she needs or wants to express. It is love she desires, she seeks acceptance from others that she comes across in her day-to-day life and she is validated by the smiles she sees on the faces of others. Even kind words cannot properly do what a smile will do in an instant.

I am a daughter of a woman with Alzheimer's disease. She sits quietly and I can see the questions in her eyes—*are you friend or foe*? I feel a deep desire to give back, even in the simplest way, to those that gave me life; the ones that nurtured me.

It's my smile she understands. Life may be filled with ups and downs, but with the grace of God I will walk my destined path to serve and impart a smile to those that walked the halls before me. I will leave my problems in the hands of God and try to bring smiles to those that need it the most.

*Jacqueline Lamica*

# Woods Woman

Slowly creeping at first, like the moss that covers naked rocks, she sweeps across the bed of pine needles. Making a pathway through the tall pine forest. Only to skip across the spring fed creek, a journey through-out the dawn. Little pearls of water droplets are forming on the wild flower petals, waking up to take a morning sip. She laces her way through the lush ivy in search of medicinal herbs, roots for the soul and sweet fragrances.

She whisks under the willows to another find, a cherished treasure. A rock caught her eye—the sparkle she could sense from within. A geode of light disguised underneath the gnarly exterior. An extraordinary gift of energy to use for special treatments. Healings which banish the darkness out of the heart. She holds this piece up into the new forming sunrise light to charge with energy for the home journey. Then, placing the treasure into her satchel, she wanders once again.

She continues as the chatter of the birds keeps her company. A woodpecker is feeding in the distance. She meanders around the ironwood, sycamores and stops at the sassafras tree to gently pick a few branches for the handmade willow basket of herbs she's been carrying to make teas. She watches the sparkle playing across the lake, only to be paused by the blooming water lilies. A great blue heron sweeps down into the tall reeds of cat tails and pussy willows.

She carries on with her journey to gather the rest of the sunny morning.

*Edda Fretz*

# Fly Away and Dance

*Written for my daughter Kristen (Krissy) Ruth Greenleaf*

My tiny little bundle, sweet child from above
that moment when your eyes met mine
I knew no greater love

Soon pitter-patter toddler feet ran nimbly through the house
soft handprints stamped the windows
by my winsome little mouse

When kindergarten time arrived you hardly made a fuss
while I wiped your tears, you smiled, we kissed
then I helped you board the bus

Your elementary, middle grades and high school years neared fast
today a college graduate
how quickly time has passed

And now that you have spread your wings it's time for you to fly
that doesn't mean you won't be back
it doesn't mean goodbye

It's just that now the choice is *yours* to *make* your dreams come true
to find and guard that sacred space
where *you* must trust in you

Remember when you wished upon the stars up in the sky?
Well I saw those dreams you wished for
as they twirled inside your eyes

And now my babe, the time has come to let you fly away
your journey will begin now
and this is what I pray

May God's great love and guiding light shine bright along the way
in which you take to learn of life
grow wiser day by day

Fly away and dance!


*Louise Huey Greenleaf*

## Bless the Broken Road

*God blessed the broken road that led me straight to you.*

There are many kinds of love. I believe it takes time and experience to tell the difference.

I married young because I thought I was in love. Looking back, I recognize it was for security. I wanted the traditional family that I didn't have growing up.

There is a passionate kind of love that consumes you. You feel like you can't live without that person, but eventually you will learn to and you will understand that there is more to a relationship than passion.

Then there is the soul-mate kind of love where you feel like you have always known this person. You don't need to work at the relationship, amazingly it just happens. It is a loving connection that leaves you feeling complete. They are your soul-mate, partner, lover, and friend.

It was a long and broken road, but I was blessed with this kind of love. I married the love of my life after I decided I was alright being alone. I am thankful each day for him and the joy and love he brings to my life.

He is not my first love, but he is my greatest love.


*Rhonda Savage*

## Free Flyers

Freedom can be achieved,
when you let your mind soar ~
Let it fly.

Instead of being tied down
by mundane chains.

We must have the strength to disbelieve ~
What naysayers say, "You can't achieve."

Only then are you free from
the concrete walls the others have built.

Freedom is a feeling which comes from within.
Those who are willing to try ~ are Free to Fly.


## On the Edge

Walking a fine line.
One step is behind, gazing at the past,
the other leaping forward, reaching out
daring the unknown—excitement…
not the status quo
as if with strangers.
Letting yourself go
into a new direction.
Go with the flow.
No judgment can be made
playing with fate on the Dance Floor of Life.


*Poetry by Edda Fretz*

# Forgetting is the Best Path to Happiness

It is good to forgive, but it's even better to forgive and forget. If you say you've forgiven someone but you still hold on to the memory of what they did that upset you, you are still trapped in the past. Staying in the past drains you of your sense of aliveness.

When you forgive and forget, you can be in the present. You can live in the now. All happiness exists in the now.

No matter what happened in the past, when you forgive and forget, you have moved into acceptance. You know you are in acceptance when you can see that everything that has happened in your life was there to help you grow. When you see this, you can forget the pain of past hurts and focus on feeling grateful for the person you have become *because* you went through these trials.

*April Dodd*

# Dream With a Renewed Mind

As we chart a new course towards a dream, we may struggle as we change old habits. Frustrated, we wake up the next day to discover we are following the same path we were on the day before. In our limited view, we convince ourselves that we failed once again.

When we listen to our own critical voice we never get on to renewing our minds with fresh thoughts. It is important to seek other positive thoughts to refresh and renew our mind. Setting sail into a new dream begins with a renewed mind charted with a new perspective.

In my personal journey, I have learned that when I renew my mind and place God in the center of my life, a new JOY and purpose is discovered when I seek the dreams that God has designed for me.

As you chart a new course towards a dream, ask God to be your Guide and Traveling Companion. As you release your heart to Him, new paths will be uncovered that you never thought possible! In renewing your mind daily with His unchanging Truths, Insights from His Word will become the power that navigates you into His dreams for you.

*Beth Robbins Bontrager*

# Moving Forward

*When one door closes, another opens; but we often look so long and so regretfully upon the closed door that we do not see the one which has opened for us.*

— Alexander Graham Bell

It is human nature to dwell on negative experiences from the past. Our pain connects us and in our misery we find comradery which continues to fuel the fire of anger left buried inside. Doors may open to new opportunities, but when you are focusing on what you missed out on or lost in the past, you will not see what's right in front of you.

We live in a world of endless possibilities. The universe is always guiding us to our greater Good. It is giving us as much as we can accept. The question is, how much good are you willing to accept?

🦋 Make a conscious commitment to let go of the pain

🦋 Express your pain and your responsibility associated with it. Journal these thoughts and feelings.

🦋 Stop being a victim and stop blaming others. You have the choice to continue to feel bad about another person's actions.

🦋 Focus on the present; the here and now—the JOY!

🦋 Forgive them and forgive yourself.

*Constance Mollerstuen*

# We Only Ever Talk About Ourselves

Consider this: No matter what you say about anyone else, the only person you're really talking about is yourself. Each of us sees the world in our own way. How you perceive an experience IS the experience to you, because you defined it. Thus, what you experience is your creation, and yours alone. Since only you can know your experience, what you talk about only reveals who you are.

Remember this when you complain about another person or feel tempted to gossip. You may think you're talking about someone else, but you are not. You are merely projecting onto that person your own interpretation based on your conditioning, experiences and your opinion of yourself. Some of these ideas you may be willing to own; some of them you won't. When you judge another, you are only judging yourself—you just haven't owned the judgment yet. You have yet to claim that given the right circumstances, you can be just like them.

When we project our self-judgments onto others, we are forgetting who we really are. When we forget our Oneness with all, we feel separate. And when we buy into the illusion of separation, it is easy to pretend there is someone else out there to talk about.

*April Dodd*

# Never Too Late

Perhaps one of the saddest phrases is, "It's too late." It signals defeat and loss. How many times have you let someone convince you it was too late? Too late to go back to college, too late for love, too late to change your life. Did you just accept it and decide not to entertain that notion ever again?

Look around; the world is full of stories of those who didn't hear "It's too late" and went on to amaze and inspire the rest of us. An 80-year-old finishing their degree, a suddenly single woman traveling solo around the world, or reunited sweethearts in love for the first time in their lives.

What is your secret aspiration that you think it's just too late to do? Travel? Write? Start a new career?

This is the most exciting time to be alive, you have never been more powerful, for you can write your own story, your own plan. If it is too frightening to say it out loud, whisper it. Try it on for size.

It's never too late—you just need to get started.

*Susan Sparks*

## What Does the Soft Animal of My Body Love?

The soft animal of my body loves the sun
    warmly beaming down on my parched skin.

It loves caressing and cuddling close to those I love—
    my dog, my husband, my granddaughters.

My soft animal body loves a warm, comfortable bed or an easy chair to
    sink into. Kisses and nibbles, and tickles and laughing.

My soft animal body likes a good walk, especially when accompanied
    by an interesting partner,

And Yoga poses that say I am a warrior and change the anxious energy
    into a positive force to be reckoned with.

My body, my body!

Oh, how much I want to be fully in tune with the wisdom it offers and
    to hear its wounded memories.

How much I would like to keep it young and healthy,
    indicating that I am well;

I am loved; and I am ready for what God purposes for me.

The soft animal of my body loves community and family and friends
    holding hands in prayerful agreement that we are;

Yes; we are one and for each other and
    with each other in this dance called life.

And oh how I love to dance to a good beat or an old melody using old
    dances that my children and grandchildren, my young friends and
    their young children laugh at and call "old school."

My body, my body loves the hum of life that runs through it and the
    chill that bring goose bumps when the Spirit is near.

What does the soft animal of my body love?

It loves living and being alive!

©Therese Taylor-Stinson

# Living With a Dream In the Midst of Life Events

Having a dream in our hearts does not stop life events from happening to us. In the midst of living we must find a way for dreams to survive in spite of those moments where our hearts are so heavy that we fear we will never rise up with joy again.

Inside of ourselves we must have a *belief system* that is the foundational system that keeps all our inner soil rich with nutrients that will sustain us through the droughts of our life. It must be the system that encourages fragile seedlings to sprout from the dreams which are planted in the inner soil of *"us."*

Through my life, I have had surgeries, experienced loss of loved ones, suffered intense humiliations, discovered how devastating depression can be, and felt helpless while watching the struggles of my elderly parents. I discovered that in my weakness, my belief system in God's Word helped to keep my head above the waters of emotions that could have overtaken me. By depending on His Truth through many life events, my dream survived. In 2014, I published my first book, *Butterfly Hugs*.

God's Word gives stability amidst life's storms while freeing a heart to dream.

*Beth Robbins Bontrager*

# Five Steps You Can Take to Be More Positive

🦋 Every day, write down three things for which you are grateful.

🦋 Smile at *everyone*.

🦋 Sit outside in nature for ten minutes. Take notice of what you see and hear.

🦋 Your thoughts control your life. Choose to think loving, kind, compassionate thoughts about yourself and others.

🦋 Become your own best friend. Buy yourself something special, take time to play, sing, dance, laugh, eat your favorite food from childhood, and decide to put *your* needs *first* on the To-do List of Life.

*Constance Mollerstuen*

# Women From the Womb

Women from the womb
deep inside walls that
are shelters from those
who throw words, attitudes,
painful darts to penetrate,
to hurt, cause pain.

Strong foundation for inner strength.
The depth of safety—a place
a cave of nurturance, beginnings,
an uplifting spot for balance.

A place of birth, rebirth, growth.
An energy center where the Chi—life force
is circulating in its own rhythm.

The place that exists deep within every one of us,
to search for.

A secret garden which changes with seasons,
tender care, watered with emotions.
The garden bountiful with colors,
fragrances and soft petals.

*Edda Fretz*

# First Steps to a Dream

Dreaming can be an emotional 'mountaintop' experience where we can lose ourselves in the joy of the moment. Yet, after this joy subsides, we may become depressed when we find ourselves alone, once again, with ourselves. Do you recognize the pattern? I think we all have experienced it. The sad reality is that many of us are not happy with ourselves. We become me-centered and not *dream-centered*. We second guess the dream and begin to list the reasons why *we cannot* dream the dream.

My journey past "me" started when I began reading inspirational devotionals and God's Word. I didn't understand a lot at first but as I continued to renew my mind my heart began to change and the first steps towards liking myself began to grow.

I began to realize that when I changed my me-centered attitude to a **J**esus first, **O**thers second, and **Y**ourself last attitude, I began to find a path to true **J-O-Y**. As I discovered the **J-O-Y** of living, I began to find the **J-O-Y** in being *me*. And, once I discovered the **J-O-Y** in being *me,* I was able to take the first steps towards the **J-O-Y** of dreaming my DREAM.

*Beth Robbins Bontrager*

# SECTION THREE

## Seasons & Holidays

### *The Flower of Life*

Some believe there is a secret symbol embedded within the Flower of Life symbol that holds the most sacred patterns of the universe. It interconnects all life and existence—from atoms, molecules to planets and galaxies. The Flower of Life illustrates the connectedness of life and Spirit and is one of the strongest, most sacred geometric shapes in existence. Meditate on its significance as you color this magical form.

# The Seasons

Seasons serve as mirrors and opportunities to pull back the veil to see more clearly into one's subconscious mind and greatest desires. Some of us love the fun and playful energy of summer while others connect with the silence and cold of winter. Autumn beckons many of us with pumpkin flavors and a bountiful harvest, while spring captures the hearts of those emerging forward, birthing something new.

We can fall in love with all of the seasons or we may have our favorites. Beneath the decorations and technical meaning of the season is the opportunity to gain a deeper sense of who we are. If you resonate with a certain season, element, or moon phase, listen, inquire more, and get curious for there is insight awaiting.

If you resist a certain season, element, or moon phase do the same yet even more so—listen to that too, because it is reflecting something wonderful back to you. If you resist the cold of winter, could it be possible that it is bringing up an aspect of you that is resistant to self-inquiry? Can you sit with this and allow the winter season to prompt you to go deeper within? For another it may be the resistance of the heat of summer. Fire burns away what no longer serves and reminds us of our personal power. Perhaps we are afraid to see the light and release what is ready to be transformed.

The seasons are powerful vessels of insight that contain great wisdom for those who are willing to look within. Each season lives to teach another lesson, and offers the guidance in how to harness it. Download the free gift of my five-year moon phase calendar at melissacorter.com.

*Melissa Kim Corter*

# New Year—New Beginnings

## Hung Over

Feeling hung over? Not from a night on the town, but the hangover that comes with making grand declarations and resolutions in the face of the New Year.

Did you decide you are going to change your life simply because you wrote down some resolutions? If that little voice has already popped into your head telling you to give it up, maybe it isn't procrastination. Maybe it is a different conversation—one with the voice of reason asking, "Whose goal is it?"

Why did you decide you needed to change something? Are your friends doing it? Think back to your mother's remark in seventh grade when you wanted to do something because all the cool girls were doing it. Are your friends signing up for ultra-marathons or humanitarian trips when your idea of activity is cleaning up a roadside or sorting food at the food bank? Or maybe your idea is running an ultramarathon but your family and friends are telling you it's a crazy idea.

Whichever path it is, make sure it is really your idea; your goal, your vision, your dream. If it is, then go for it.

*Susan Sparks*

# Taking Out My Garbage

As we enter a new year, I firmly resolve that I am finally, once and for all, unpacking all of my baggage—all the hurt, disillusionment, betrayal, dysfunction, resentment, pettiness, inconsideration, anger, broken promises and failed expectations.

I place it all at the proverbial curb to be hauled away with the bulk trash. By the grace and blessing of God's greater glory, wisdom and mercy, as is with all deteriorating garbage, mine too shall fade back into the folds of the earth—and I will move forward, unencumbered by the past.

Closing this chapter, I will take up pen and fresh paper and once again be the sole author of my story, leaving behind all of its negative contributors. I wish them peace and their just rewards. My joy, smile and love shall never again be thwarted by actions beyond my control.

"Fool me once, shame on you. Fool me twice (three, four, five…times), shame on me!"

Though I have forgiven the repetitive antagonists of my life, I am no longer willing to compromise my happiness, and so I set them free. With their freedom comes my own! It is with open arms, a renewed sense of who I am and faith that I will always be given the strength of love to surmount all obstacles.

I welcome the New Year like never before. I am grateful and thankful.


*Trish Norman-Figueiredo*

# Springtime

## Spring

Water droplets melting, sliding off icicles,
awnings, tree branches
one drop at a time,
just sliding,
    drip
       ping
         down
            w
              a
               r
                d

Watering the still lightly frozen ground,
breaking the surface of wet snow
creating dimples in the earth,
puddles for splashing, drinking pools.
There is a mist in the air,

fragrant with earthy scents,
the freshness of wet ground
soaking upward into the twilight sky.
Droplets suspended in light,
glistening dewdrops
slowly falling back down washing things anew.
Preparing the soil, softening the hard landscape

for plant life to reach up, force its way out,
alive with fresh color,
accenting the subtle earth tones,
adding vibrancy to life.

*Edda Fretz*

# Spring Opens the Way

Spring opens the way for new life. Unlike the New Year which comes in with much pomp and fanfare, spring peels back the black, bleak gray pieces of winter instead. It reawakens the slumbering earth to revive and renew.

Spring is steadfast and purposeful without being overwhelming. It enters with ferocity as it fights its way through winter's final blows and bitter cold to bring warm refreshment to the soul. It brings us to a place of pleasant comfort before handing us onto the intensity of summer. Spring is a rejuvenating respite in the cycle of life.

Rejoice in renewal and the season of youthful spirit. Prepare your soul for refreshment as you go out and fiercely brave the new beginnings in your life.

*Patricia Mooneyham*

# May Day

In our mother's and grandmother's generations, May Day was a celebration of spring, renewed growth, and joy. They spread this joy by leaving small bouquets of flowers on door steps of friends, neighbors or family.

Mayday is a distress call by ships at sea or a plane in peril. While you may not be adrift at sea, you may feel adrift in life, disconnected from loved ones, your dreams or your faith. Does it feel that no one hears your Mayday call?

Maybe the best way is to answer your own distress call. Celebrate May Day. Spread some joy. Look around and notice the warmer days, the greening of the earth, and the beauty of flowers. Surprise someone with a small bouquet hung on their front door, take a walk or give them your full attention for a change.

When you look for ways to spread joy to others, the distress call fades away. There is no need for a search and rescue party, unless of course, it is to celebrate your own.

*Susan Sparks*

# A Summer Celebration

Oh, to savor the warming days of summer! Rejoice at the return of the light when Mother Earth is bountiful with color and bursting with the fruits of her labor.

Today, I breathe in new life and release the dark days of winter's repose. May I be inspired by summer breezes felt lightly on my skin as if kissed by angels on the wind.

I embrace the fruit of earth's healing abilities as I am surrounded by lush meadows and rich farmlands. I am joyfully immersed in the feel of the earth beneath my feet and the grass tickling me between my toes.

I relish the twinkling lights in a summer night's starry sky. Its timeless constellations guide me as I navigate the journey ahead with the promise of daylight not far beyond. I pray that the path will be well lit before me in this life.

I invoke the protection and support of my Creator whose radiant presence is as wide as the clear blue sky—and as infinite as well. I am lovingly reminded that the only limitations in this life are those which I place upon myself.

Let me dance forever in the days and bask in the luminous glow of a summer's moon—and know that, for all time, all is well in my world.

Amen.

*Connie Gorrell*

## Autumn is the Season of Fulfillment

As the colors of the trees turn to bold reds and golds and the final days of the harvest bring us closer to the year's end, it is a time to look at the successes and changes of the months gone by. Before the rush of the holiday season and the cold, quiet rest of winter hibernation, autumn is a time to celebrate family and fulfillment.

The clear blue skies of October afternoons and the just right cool of the late afternoons frees the mind to hold hands with Mother Nature as she paints the world in fiery colors. Bonfires and boots bring people together after the lazy ways of wandering through summer days and nights. Old souls roam free on All Hallows Eve.

As we remember those we know we will see again, we build our treasure trove as we march on toward giving thanks.

Let your cup runneth over with gratitude and plenty during this season of fulfillment.

*Patricia Mooneyham*

# Thankful Only Once a Year?

Sandwiched between Trick-or-Treat and Christmas is a date that is becoming nothing short of a blip on the shopping radar. Thanksgiving. When you stop and think about it, a day to concentrate on being thankful pulls at our hungry hearts more than the lure of roast turkey, football, and shopping mayhem. But like all things quiet and still, it is often lost to us by the noisier call of the world. Some are able to stop and be thankful on that one day before racing out to other activities. But why be thankful only once a year?

Imagine how full your heart can be if you take time to concentrate on being thankful every day. Despite having a bad day, sickness or sadness in your life, you can muster one thing to be thankful for. Challenge yourself to find something every day. Start a list, stuff them in a jar or a journal and on the one day when the rest of your family and friends are cramming all their gratitude into one day, you'll have 365 days of gratitude to savor again.

*Susan Sparks*

# Winter Solstice

A time for reflection,
inner soul journeys merge with memories.

The longest night of the year to dream,
make wishes and confer with guides.

Midnight meditations, candlelight and star bright.

Whispers in the chilly breeze,
a crack in the woods and squeaks in the snow.

Embers in a fire pit, pops in a wood stove, a whistle of a tea
kettle.

Softness of grandmother quilts made long ago,
treasures of special times.

*Edda Fretz*

# Enjoy the Journey

We wish you well on as you revel in your journey of confidence, courage, strength and Light. There comes a celebratory moment when we realize just how wonderfully unique our sacred essence. That time for you is *now*. There is no better time.

Woman to woman, today we commit to end comparisons in our life. We perceive another as being confident, strong, and having it all together. Sure, she may *appear* to be the elegant swan, effortlessly gliding atop cool, peaceful waters—when really, below the surface, she is paddling wildly just trying to keep up. I imagine others perceive you and me to be the cool, calm and collected ones—only, we know the truth! We are in this thing together.

Hear me when I tell you that joy is simply your *inner light*. It is the light instilled in you from the beginning. The illuminating light that shined within you when your children were born, when you fell in love, or even now when music fills your dreams. Be open and willing to receive all the little joys life has to offer.

There is beauty in letting go of what no longer serves you. Let go of pain or the shame of past mistakes or of memories that invade your sleep at night. Wake up to realize that your dreams are patiently waiting for you—waiting to hear you say, "Enough! I can do better than this...*and I will*."

Be on your way now. Reach for the stars, for I am truly convinced that they are reaching back.

You've got this!

*Connie Gorrell*

The *Gift* of *Inspiration* for *Women*
*is your constant companion!*

The following blank pages are for your journal entries. Use them to write your thoughts or list the page numbers of your favorite passages so you can find them easily and read them again and again, whenever you need a touch of inspiration.

Page numbers for my favorite passages are:

My inspirations:

My inspirations:

My inspirations:

# THE *Mission;*

The DreamSTRONG Foundation is a platform for women, women-owned businesses and communities working toward prosperity through inspiration, education and social justice for women and girls. Our mission is to strengthen women's voices, enrich the lives of those in need by cultivating leadership, education, philanthropy, and respect for all women. Through our programs created specifically for the needs of women, DreamSTRONG™ is building a strong foundation for the future of women and families in all walks of life.

**www.dreamstrong.org**

Made in the USA
Charleston, SC
27 November 2016